Purify Your Body

Purify Your Body

Natural Remedies for Detoxing from 50 Everyday Situations

Nina L. Diamond

CROWN TRADE PAPERBACKS

NEW YORK

Published by Crown Trade Paperbacks, 201 East 50th Street, New York,
New York 10022. Member of the Crown Publishing Group.

Random House, Inc. New York, Toronto, London, Sydney, Auckland
http://www.randomhouse.com/
CROWN TRADE PAPERBACKS and colophon are trademarks of Crown
Publishers, Inc.

Printed in the United States of America

Design by Cathryn S. Aison

Library of Congress Cataloging-in-Publication Data
Diamond, Nina L.
Purify your body : natural remedies for detoxing from 50
everyday situations / by Nina L. Diamond.
p.   cm.
Includes index.
1. Stress management.   2. Detoxification. Metabolic.   3. Alternative
medicine.   4. Stress (Physiology)   I. Title.
RA785.D428   1997
613—dc20   96-29190
CIP

ISBN 0-517-88745-2 (pbk.)

10 9 8 7 6 5 4 3 2 1

FIRST EDITION

To the "impatient patient," who doesn't know
that he's also a healer,

AND

to the memory of Abe Einhorn, Morris Plotnick, Louis
Plotnick, and Sally Rothery.

AUTHOR'S NOTE

This book is not intended as a substitute for the medical advice of physicians, nor is it meant to encourage diagnosis and treatment of illness, disease, or other medical problems by the layman. The reader should consult his or her physician before trying any of the treatments contained in this book.

CONTENTS

ACKNOWLEDGMENTS

When the editors at Harmony suggested this book, they didn't realize that it had been growing in my filing cabinets and in my mind for many years. As a journalist covering alternative medicine, natural healing, medical research, the arts and sciences, metaphysics, and spirituality, my research, article, and interview files were secretly organizing themselves all along, so that when the opportunity arose, I was ready to begin the process of creating a book like this.

With twenty years' worth of magazine and newspaper editors, colleagues, and friends to thank for their skill, trust, support, and friendship, I'd like to specifically give a big thanks to *Omni* magazine's Rob Killheffer, Kathleen Stein, and Anna Copeland Wheatley; *Longevity* magazine's John Tarkov and Marie Hodge; the *Miami Herald Health Beat*'s Marilyn Moore; the *Fort Lauderdale Sun Sentinel*'s/*Sunshine Magazine*'s John Parkyn, Mark Gauert, and Cheryl Frost; *Body Mind Spirit* magazine's Carol Kramer and Rochelle Gordon; the *Chicago Tribune*'s Marjorie David; *South Florida* magazine's staff from "the good ol' days"—Maureen Glabman, Rick Eyerdam, J.P. Faber, Bonnie Lewis, photographer Steve Nelson, and the founding family of extraordinary journalists, Sylvan and Anne Meyer, and Erica M. Rauzin. If I could wish anything for fellow journalists and writers, it would be that they have an editor and friend like Erica in their lives. Not a day goes by when I don't hearken back to something she taught me or pass her wisdom along to a writer I am coaching or editing.

Also, a hearty thanks to my friends and colleagues whose insight, knowledge, love, and support have been instrumental in my work. You all know that I could not have written this book without you:

Pam Johnson, Gladys Seymour Davis, James Redfield, Howard Libin, Mindi Rudan, Laura Jacobs, Timolin Cole Augustus, Matthew Glassman, Diane Batshaw Eisman, M.D., Eugene Eisman, M.D., Dwight Lauderdale, Marilyn Sunderman, Elyktra Eisman, Deborah Mash, Ph.D., Brooke Medicine Eagle, Gary Wilson, Michelle Newman, Kathryn and Rob Cowdery, Heidi ("Dr. Rat") and Joe Camilli, Naomi Otterbein Bryant, Jonathan Ellis, Lisa Beane Goldman, David Glabman, M.D., David and Christine Perry, Steve Perry, Lorrie Robinson, Anne Sellaro, Brian Weiss, M.D., Jim Brosemer, Christine DeLorey, Juanita Mazzarella, and all the Pandas.

The spirit, wisdom, contributions, and humor of each one of you is represented in this book.

Thank you to my extended family: Bob and Debbie, Erica, Randi and Jacob Diamond; my cat, the irrepressible Jessie; Edie and Marty Bruckner; Carol and Aaron Friedman; and Lil and Mickey Cohen, for your encouragement, love, and support.

To my colleagues on the Chopra newsletter at Crown: Deepak Chopra, M.D., Patty Eddy, Lyn Garrison, and the staff, thank you for your endless stream of information and support.

Special thanks to my agent, Lynn Franklin, for bringing this opportunity to me and to her associate Masha Alexander.

And, finally, to my editor, Sherri Rifkin, my heartfelt thanks for your creative skills, trust, and friendship, especially as I neared my manuscript deadline and thought I might actually be living out every chapter of this book.

Introduction

*I*t's time to destroy the myths and straighten out the misconceptions that even the most well-educated and health-conscious among us may have.

Mention the word *detox,* and you're likely to be met by this comment: "Oh, you're talking about enemas, right? Well, I'm regular, first thing in the morning like clockwork, so that's all I need to be concerned with, right?"

Well, not exactly. That's just the last leg of *one* of the body's detox journeys. Thinking that regular bowel movements are the only way of detoxing the body would be like believing that your car's systems are all running smoothly and efficiently just because there's exhaust coming out of the tailpipe. Being regular is great, but it doesn't mean that your lymphatic or circulation systems are functioning at optimum levels, or that your liver isn't overburdened and therefore unable to process toxins effectively, or that the inflammation or degenerative disease hasn't impaired the efficiency of your joints.

This book's objective is to demystify the processes involved in ridding your body of the natural and manmade toxins it encounters and, by providing prevention and treatment techniques, guide you through the many health-giving and healing ways to keep your systems running smoothly. The antidotes you'll find here are gentle, natural, and balanced—and have nothing to do with blasting out your digestive and elimination systems.

First, we have to define what detoxing actually is: Detoxing is ridding the body of the effects of what's been brought into it from the outside, as well as ridding it of what's been created from the inside as a result of daily use, stress, and burdening of the body's various systems and organs by a variety of factors.

Everything from the outside that interacts with your body has a profound effect on it—physically, emotionally, and spiritually. The same goes for everything churning around, doing its job, or being created *inside* your body. Sometimes the effect can be toxic, meaning injurious to your health, ranging from a mild, cumulative reaction to a severe one, and deriving from environmental toxins, food toxins, and even toxic relationships.

What can we do to prevent exposure to various kinds of toxins? What can we do to make sure the body rids itself of external toxins? What are the cumulative effects of external toxins? How can we reduce these effects, treat them, counteract them? You will find the answers here. And don't worry, it's not nearly as scary as it sounds.

Your body also creates toxic effects internally when systems are impaired—by everything from ordinary daily use and function to illness, reaction to medications, allergy, age, chemical imbalance, nutritional deficiencies, lack of exercise, lifestyle factors, and stress. You will learn how to identify these internal processes and increase your awareness of what you can do, safely and naturally, to help your body counteract anything that could cause a problem.

Taking care of your body also means taking care of your mind and spirit, which affect the well-being of your physical form, and vice versa. Stresses or impairment in any one area has a profound effect on the other two.

Do you live in the city, the suburbs, or a more rural setting? Where and how you live affects your physical, emotional, and spiritual health, and therefore your body's ability to detox itself.

You may not realize that your stress level at work and at home is affecting you. This book will explain what part stress plays in your body's and mind's ability to detox itself and what you can do to help the process. Are you getting enough sleep? Do you hold your emotions in or can you express them easily? What part does nutrition play in your health and your body's ability to detox naturally? Every conceivable lifestyle and general health issue registers with your entire being.

In Part One of this book, you'll learn how your body's systems work when they are running free of impairments and are able to detox as they were designed to do. You'll take a grand tour of the circulatory, respiratory, immune, digestive, urinary, endocrine, reproductive, and nervous systems and consider your organs, skin, bones, muscles, teeth, eyes, ears, throat, and nose.

In Part Two, you'll be introduced to the basics of natural (often referred to as "alternative") medicine as we explore bodywork, aromatherapy and essential oils, herbs and botanicals, vitamins, nutrition, acupuncture and acupressure, meditation, vibrational medicine, Ayurveda, Chinese Medicine, Native American and other native cultures' healing practices, among other such scientifically researched, proven and time-honored methods.

In Part Three, which makes up the heart of the book, you'll learn how to stay healthy, with all your systems running smoothly, efficiently, and consistently. You'll be surprised, perhaps, at how really easy it is to do this, how good it feels, and how life altering it can be. You'll see how natural prevention and healing methods affect your body, mind, and spirit, focusing on how they apply to detoxification, and therefore restoring balance, proper function, and, in many cases, peace of mind. In this guide to fifty everyday personal, physical, emotional, and lifestyle situations that can stress the body, mind, and spirit, you'll learn about natural treatments and practices as you discover how these can help you as preventive measures and antidotes in each particular situation.

Everyone is faced with so many of these fifty situations—it is called *life*. From lack of sleep, work stress, jet lag, and environmental toxins to injury, addiction, illness, and toxic household cleaning products, you'll find situations specific to men and women, stages of life, adventurers, country folks and city folks, occupations, hobbies, sports, and activities.

In each of ten categories in Part Three, you'll find the fifty situations presented in detailed yet easy to understand explanations of cause and effect, prevention, and antidotes. One situation in each category, chosen because it is so common and regularly affects so many of us, is spotlighted for a bit of extra attention.

One of the goals of this book is to make you think about your health in ways that may be new to you. One of the aspects of natural health is the idea of "cleaning up after yourself," as one wise bodywork therapist I know calls it. That means that if you like to have a glass of wine with dinner on occasion, you can certainly enjoy it, and perhaps even with less guilt, because after reading this book you'll know what to do to help reduce the toxic effects alcohol has on your body.

This book does *not* condone neglecting or damaging your health. If you smoke, you don't need any more lectures about the dangers, but you *do* need to know how you can counteract some of the damage that smoking causes until you can quit. This book encourages you to let go of toxic habits and to be aware of toxic situations and how you can prevent and treat them. Some situations are very easy to remedy. You can remove most pesticides from your life, for example, simply by buying only organic produce and not eating processed foods. Other situations, like addiction, or exposure to environmental or occupational toxins, are more difficult to treat or prevent.

The book ends with an extensive resource list. It shows where to find more information about natural treatments and toxic situations in helpful books, publications, and tapes and through professional organizations and companies that provide products and services.

As a journalist, I've compiled this information from research and interviews with scientists, alternative/natural medicine pioneers, researchers, physicians, health care practioners, healers, environmental experts, and visionaries of all kinds.

My motivation as a writer and information junkie (I don't think I've ever found any antidote for this particular addiction) is quite simple: I'm incredibly curious. It comes naturally to me to express that curiosity creatively, on paper, out loud, and in the music I compose. Simultaneously drawn to the arts and sciences, I remember when the two merged for me for the first time. I was probably no more than eight years old, taking piano lessons from a teacher whose son and daughter I knew from the neighborhood and school. One afternoon, my lesson completed, I went upstairs in their house to play with them. One suggested we "play doctor." Looking back now, I realize that many children used that phrase to mean the innocent peeking inside of clothes that boys and girls do when they're quite young and curious, but at the time, that never even crossed my mind. Delighted to "play doctor," I dashed into their hallway bathroom and returned with my little arms full of supplies and proceeded to tend to their imaginary wounds with Band-Aids, Ace bandages, tape, gauze, and slings. When I was finished with them they both looked like extras from the Civil War hospital scenes in *Gone with the Wind*. I don't think it was exactly what they had in mind, but I took "playing doctor" quite literally and took pride in my delicate handiwork and compassionate bedside manner. They never asked me to play doctor again.

Medical terminology was used quite freely around my house when I was growing up. My father had wanted to be a doctor. He had also wanted to be a painter. Ultimately, he chose neither as a career and became a business owner instead. But my own exposure to both the creative arts and healing would ultimately unite in my career.

My father quit smoking in 1960, before we were encouraged to do so. He had books on medicine, but also on yoga. He was a "health nut," to use the term used in those days before there was widespread interest in actively taking part in your own health care, and I'd go with him to one of the few stores that specialized in vitamins, supplements, and health foods. I would listen intently as he explained it all to me.

Even when I was very young, healing fascinated me, and I was particularly drawn to natural approaches. Childhood bouts with tonsilitis convinced me that there had to be more to health and healing than what mainstream medicine could provide. Because I have always been slim (thanks to genetics and a quick metabolism), I didn't react to medications the way other people did. I was overly sensitive to them, requiring smaller doses, and I noticed that most mainstream physicians prescribed as if you were some generic humanoid, with no thought to the particulars of your size and systems. So, I began to "play doctor" with the doctors. I became my own co-doctor, reminding them of my particular sensitivities, suggesting alternate approaches, and often successfully diagnosing myself. After all, I knew my body better than they did and certainly had more time to play detective with my symptoms and possible causes—I didn't have another patient I had to get to in five minutes. Along the way, I asked a lot of questions, researched, read, watched documentaries, and pondered a lot, exploring all facets of mainstream and alternative medicine, prevention, and philosophies.

I found that when something physical was amiss, doctors wanted to give me a prescription and send me on my way. But I wasn't interested in that. It was my body and I wanted to know *why* something was wrong and how I could actually fix it, not just mask the symptoms. On more than one occasion, not delighted by what a doctor wanted to do, I literally *willed* myself better in order to avoid what I considered harmful or painful medical intervention.

Asking what was involved in the process of performing a root canal about a dozen years ago (it was my first one, and I was curious), I found myself, in effect, interviewing my dentist while I sat in the chair going numb from the novocaine.

"What, are you writing a book?" he responded sarcastically.

Clearly, he wasn't used to patients wanting to know the step-by-step procedure. I told him that my philosophy is simple: the more I know, the better I can take care of myself, and even make his job easier.

A few months ago, visiting his office for a routine cleaning, I told him that I was writing this book. He wasn't surprised, and he asked for a copy. I hope I'm no longer one of a few patients who ask questions of their dentists and physicians.

Instead of leaving it all in the hands of the men and women in the white coats, we, as a society, have become more involved in the care of our bodies and beings in the last decade. We're in the process of coming full circle: Native American medicine men used to go live with a member of the tribe who needed healing in order to factor in their relationships and daily routine into diagnosis and treatment; the patient was then taught the healing ways he or she needed to know. Country doctors may not have actually moved in, but they took the same approach with their patients and their expertise was greatly supplemented by healing ways practiced at home, known then as "folk cures" or "home remedies." You may remember some of these, passed down from your parents or grandparents.

In our home, when I was growing up, we relied a lot on chicken soup to help us through colds and the flu. A few years ago, researchers at the University of Nebraska Medical Center in Omaha found the scientific evidence to back up the healing effects of this ancient home remedy. A combination of chicken and vegetables (you need both—chicken or vegetables alone won't do the trick) in soup inhibits the movement of neutrofils, which are white blood cells that fight infection by releasing enzymes that attack invading bacteria or viruses. Unfortunately, these enzymes also attack the body's harmless cells, and that's what causes inflammation, which expresses itself as cold and flu symptoms such as stuffy and runny nose, swollen sinuses, inflamed lung tissue, aches, and the like. Apparently, the vegetables in broth are actually what inhibit the movement of these infection fighting white cells, which by itself isn't really such good news because although we would like to do without the inflammation, we certainly don't want to do without the great thing these white cells do, which is fight infection. Here's where the chicken comes in. The chicken in the soup helps the white blood cells continue fighting the infection, while the veggies keep the white blood cells from causing inflammation. An amazing feat.

Over the years, my interest in healing led me to incorporate it into my work as a journalist and writer. My curiosity about what makes people tick, and how they creatively express themselves in the arts and the media, led me to cover those areas in hundreds of magazine and newspaper feature articles. Then I found that my curiosity about what makes our bodies and spirits tick was leading me to write less about the arts, media, and other areas, and more about science, medical research, alternative medicine, the mind-body connection, metaphysics, and spirituality. The transition was natural and smooth, given my lifelong interest and research, and now it has been my main journalistic focus for the better part of a decade.

I've found out that exploring the body, mind, and spirit is one of the most rewarding things a curious information junkie can do. In passing along this information, I hope to instill in you that same curiosity, so that it may empower you in your personal health care.

Writing this book, I discovered that *everything* our bodies do or we do in order to facilitate healing involves the detoxification process. It's the natural order of the world to seek balance. You know—"In with the good, out with the bad." Detoxing is one of your body's primary functions. Without this inherent ability, none of us would have lived past our first breath, because we exhale carbon dioxide!

None of this is mysterious or complicated, and you may even find as you're reading along that you are already doing great things for yourself that detox. There's an old saying that anything that tastes good or feels good is probably bad for you. Well, think again. This book is filled with easy, inexpensive, time-efficient, painless, pleasurable things that taste good, feel good, and can make you very healthy. And happy, too.

How to Use This Book

To get the most out of this book, I recommend that you read Parts One and Two first before looking up any of the particular situations in Part Three. The first two parts, which are brief, will give you important information that will help you better understand the causes and effects, preventive measures and antidotes, discussed in the situations in Part Three, which goes into greater detail about the nature of individual natural treatments.

Once you're in Part Three, I recommend that you read the All-Purpose Antidotes entry, which appears before the chapters on the situations on page 55. These All-Purpose Antidotes will help you as preventives and antidotes in each of the fifty situations. I will remind you throughout Part Three when to use the All-Purpose Antidotes, and which ones in particular are especially beneficial to the situation. For each situation, I provide many *other* preventive measures and antidotes that are especially beneficial in the specific case. Because so many of life's situations overlap—stress, for example, is a major component in plenty of other situations besides the situation of stress itself—there are several cross-references to other entries.

In chapter X, Times of Life, I give you a brief overview of how the stages of life generally affect your health in terms of unique physical, emotional, or spiritual stresses or susceptibility to toxic activity within your body, mind, or spirit. The Annual Physicals Timeline at the end of that chapter will remind you of some of the basics in diagnostic testing and evaluation that are suggested for the various ages and stages of your life.

Each of the fifty situations discussed in Part Three have many components and many situations within them, which are either expressly stated or implied. For instance, literally millions of life's little (and big!) annoyances can be dealt with by following the ideas and suggestions in chapter II, Emotional and Spiritual Stress, in section 8, Anxiety, Worry, and Fear.

If while reading anything in this book you think to yourself, "I'd like to know more about this," or "Where can I find these products?" or "How can I find a naturopathic, holistic, or particular type of physician, health care practitioner, or treatment therapist?" consult Resources at the end of the book.

PART ONE

How Your Body Works

The body has its own self-cleaning, self-purifying systems; the best way to protect yourself from toxicity is to keep those systems in good working order.
—Andrew Weil, M.D.

Getting to Know Your Body

$\mathcal{M}$ost of us probably know more about how our cars and computers work than how our bodies do. Usually, it's only when something goes wrong that we even think about the 24-hours-a-day operation of our systems or a particular part. And then, unfortunately, we often just plunk ourselves down on an examining table and say to the doctor, "Fix this," without knowing very much about what "this" is, or why we've got a problem with it.

Many of us treat our cars and computers much better than we treat our own bodies. We read manuals about our machines, learn everything we can, take a host of preventative measures to ensure that they run properly and won't let us down when we need them most, lovingly pamper and clean them, listen attentively for every noise that shouldn't be there, and act quickly when even the smallest thing goes wrong.

Of course, our emotional relationships with our machines are quite different from the ones we have with our bodies. Nobody would ever pretend that there was nothing wrong with the computer or the car, but, out of fear, we do an awful lot of pretending when it comes to our bodies. We're afraid of the worst—afraid of death, disability, lingering illness, pain, inconvenience. There's no reason to live in fear of our bodies. Sure, they're magical, mystical, mysterious, even miraculous, but just like your car and computer, the more you know about them, the better off you'll be.

With that in mind, let's take a grand tour of your body. As you get to know your body, keep in mind that the main organs of detoxification—those that bear most of the burden of the detox process—are the skin, lungs, liver, kidneys, and intestines.

To detoxify is to heal, and to heal is to detoxify.

The Circulatory System

*L*ike every other system in your body, the circulatory system is all about balance: giving you what you need and removing what you don't need.

In the "what you need" department, your heart pumps blood to the lungs, where the blood receives oxygen. In the "what you don't need" department, when the blood reaches the lungs, it gives up carbon dioxide, which is partially waste produced by the body's cells and partially used by your body to control your overall acid/alkaline balance. The freshly oxygenated blood returns to the heart, then goes out through the aorta, your main artery, and travels on to all the other arteries, which feed into the blood vessels that carry blood throughout your body.

The good stuff/bad stuff exchange finishes in the capillaries, your tiniest blood vessels, where once again oxygen is delivered, but now also nutrients from the blood travels as well. And, again, carbon dioxide and other waste products are picked up and continue their journey toward eventual release from your body.

Your blood is in continuous flow as it is recycled throughout the body. Red blood cells carry oxygen from the lungs to all of your tissues, and white blood cells protect the body from anything it considers to be an inside or outside invader, attacking, killing, and producing antibodies to neutralize or kill those invaders.

"The whole system is in homeostatic balance," says Eugene Eisman, M.D., cardiologist, internist, and co-author with his wife, Diane, a family practice physician, of *Your Child and Cholesterol*. He explains just how remarkably the body's "automatic pilot" operates: "Blood vessels are surrounded by muscles—controlled by various nerves and hormones—and these muscles control which organs and areas get which portion of the body's blood. It's distributed just right. That way, when you stand up, it all doesn't drain down to your left big toe."

The brain gets the largest portion of blood, with the other major organs each receiving a substantial amount. The kidneys alone get about 20 percent of the blood supply.

Anything that weakens or damages the heart will affect its ability to pump blood properly, and anything that impairs the arteries or blood vessels affects their ability to circulate blood throughout your body. Your body needs to be able to distribute oxygen and nutrients freely and to collect waste matter for eventual elimination.

What can go wrong? Congenital defects, stress, injuries, and disease can cause quite an unappealing array of heart and circulatory problems, including: irregular heartbeat, heart disease, heart attack, clogged arteries, blood clots, high blood pressure, low blood pressure, stroke, anemia, gangrene, aneurysms, embolisms, hemorrhages, and blood diseases and disorders. Even varicose veins and cold extremities are signs of circulatory problems.

High blood pressure is an example of one of the body's sneaky maneuvers, an abnormality that we can't see or feel but can be detected and measured by instruments. "The first external sign that you have high blood pressure would be a stroke or a heart attack, so that's why having your blood pressure routinely checked is a good idea," says Dr. Eisman.

Circulation also controls core body temperature, keeping it constant by allowing portions of blood to go just under the skin's surface in order to radiate heat out of the body. In cold weather we'll have cold skin, hands, feet, and nose because our blood vessels constrict near the skin's surface (especially in the extremities), in order to send more blood to our body's interior, where that extra warmth is urgently needed in our organs.

Overheating or a hot flash works in the opposite way. Blood vessels just under the skin's surface open wide (due to a variety of causes, including hormone fluctuations, and physical exertion), thus allowing more blood to occupy each vessel. The heat from the blood radiates out of the body, away from our organs, making us feel very warm.

Like the rest of your body, the circulatory system is designed to automatically balance itself. You can picture this beautifully intricate maze as a flowing landscape of rivers, streams, and creeks that must be free of obstruction, disease, and toxins in order to stay healthy and life-supporting.

The Respiratory System

In every ancient healing tradition, breath is revered as the life force, because without air, we could not live. As you'll recall from our first stop on this tour, your heart pumps blood to the lungs, where the blood receives life-giving oxygen and disposes of toxic carbon dioxide. The mechanics of this swap, however, is the job of the respiratory system, and it happens automatically with each breath.

You can inhale through either your nose or mouth, but when air enters your body through your nose, you receive the added benefits of your nose's job, which is to warm, moisten, and filter the air before it moves down your throat. Every child has heard Mom yell, "Don't pick your nose!"—but removing those particles (admittedly best done with a tissue and not your finger) is actually a healthy act of detoxification. It's those little nose hairs that help trap tiny particles you've inhaled and keep them from going any farther than your nose.

Once air has traveled down your throat, it quickly passes your larynx (the "voice box" that vibrates when making speech) and goes into your trachea, appropriately referred to as the windpipe, which, at its end, divides into bronchi, air passages that connect it to the lungs. Inside each lung the bronchi further divide into bronchioles, smaller and smaller airways, which look remarkably like tree roots. At the end of the tiniest bronchioles, little sacs called alveoli play host to the exchange of oxygen for carbon dioxide. Oxygen leaves the sacs and enters the blood via tiny blood vessels. Carbon dioxide leaves the bloodstream and, after passing through the alveoli sacs, is ultimately exhaled.

When we inhale and exhale, our lungs expand and contract by the action of a muscle just under the chest called the diaphragm and by subsequent motion of the rib cage. When your diaphragm contracts (and the chest cage diameter increases), the air pressure inside your chest is reduced to less than the air pressure outside your body, and this draws air into your lungs, an inhalation. When your diaphragm expands and relaxes, air is pushed out of your lungs, an exhalation.

Anything that irritates, harms, or weakens the lungs, the bronchi, the alveoli, or any other component of the respiratory system can alter your ability to breathe fully and properly, and to deliver oxygen to the blood and release carbon dioxide, resulting in conditions such as pneumonia, asthma, bronchitis, pleurisy, embolism, tuberculosis, upper respiratory infection, apnea (breathing interruption), and benign and malignant tumors.

The Immune System

The immune system is your body's protection, defense, and resistance force. When we talk about this system, we often use images and analogies that sound more like team sports or war than the round-the-clock internal activities of your body. We say that our immune system "defends against attacking invaders." These invaders could be anything the body sees as harmful, from bacteria and viruses and other external agents to internal entities, such as cancer cells, with the potential to cause illness or malfunction. When we get a cold or flu, we say, "My resistance was down," meaning our resistance to harmful organisms or substances.

How does our immune system work? With its own version of weapons. When an invader, an antigen, attacks from within or from the outside, the immune system's lymph system produces antibodies. These specialized proteins have a variety of functions that enable them to destroy or neutralize antigens, which may be bacteria, viruses, or other so-called foreign substances. The body also elevates its production of white blood cells to combat the invaders.

Most of the time, once antibodies have been created to fight a particular invader, that invader will not be detrimental to the body again. That's when we say we're *immune* to something, and it's why, for instance, we don't catch the same cold twice. Each time we get a cold, it is caused by a different virus. Once antibodies against it have been created, they continue to circulate throughout your body and will protect you from that particular invader if it attacks again. Measles is another example of a disease that you won't catch twice.

Sometimes, though, antibodies get confused about their duties and are created in order to fight something that isn't a harmful invader, like pollen or another substance, and you develop an allergy. The allergy is caused by antibodies fighting something as if it were a germ threat. As a result, all kinds of fighting symptoms arise, such as sneezing, congestion, sore throat, hives, digestive problems. Virtually any kind of symptom that mimics a symptom of an illness or disease can actually be an allergic reaction. Antibodies are also behind the rejection of transplanted organs. The body knows something foreign has been introduced, and the immune system makes antibodies to fight this foreign object, as if it were something harmful, though it isn't. Antibodies also play a role in blood transfusions. If the wrong type of blood is given to you, your body will make antibodies to destroy it.

The lymph system, your body's drainage system, is also part of the immune system. The system is comprised of a vast network of lymph vessels that carry excess fluid, waste, and toxins from everywhere in your body and send them to be ultimately eliminated via your blood circulation. The lymph nodes, also referred to as lymph glands, are located on either side of your neck; under your jaw; under the armpits near the sides of the breasts; where each thigh meets your torso in the groin area; and in the upper part of your chest. The lymph glands' chief function is to filter the lymph fluid. Special white blood cells in your lymph glands surround and kill any harmful bacteria, viruses, or other nasty organisms that come through, which is why when you are ill you might have swollen glands. This is the white blood cells at work destroying the germs before the lymph fluid goes back out into the bloodstream.

Problems with your immune system include: allergies, autoimmune diseases (in which antibodies attack the body's own tissues), Acquired Immune Deficiency Syndrome (AIDS), and lowered resistance to illness.

The Digestive System

Digestion can be summed up simply: Food goes in; waste goes out. In between, your body converts the food into fuel for itself, based on the particular nutrients you've digested. Once your body absorbs these nutrients, the residue passes through the bowel. If you are healthy, you should eliminate solid waste one to three times per day, depending on how much you eat. If the waste isn't going out of you often enough, it putrefies, and toxins make their way into all of your organs, causing the beginning of a degenerative disease.

Here's how food makes the trip through your body: First it enters your mouth, where it's ground by your teeth and mixed with saliva secreted by glands in your mouth. Your saliva contains an enzyme (a specialized protein) that begins to chemically break down the starches in what you are chewing. You swallow the food; it goes into the esophagus, then to the stomach. Acid and digestive juices containing enzymes mix in with the food, reducing it to a semifluid state so it can go on to the small intestine. In the small intestine, the digestive juices from your liver and pancreas break down the food mixture into nutrients, which will be absorbed into your bloodstream in the lower part of your small intestine.

The liver also produces bile, which is required for fats to be absorbed while they're being processed in the small intestine. The liver also removes wastes from the blood, produces and stores the sugar and glucose, and processes many medications. Your gallbladder, which is under your liver, stores the bile that the liver makes, and releases it as needed into the small intestine. The pancreas secretes digestive juices that the small intestine needs to digest and absorb fats and starches. The pancreas, just behind the stomach, also secretes hormones, including insulin, which helps the body absorb and use glucose sugar.

Anything that hasn't been absorbed into your bloodstream through the small intestine moves on to the large intestine. There, this waste is processed into feces, while water and chemicals are absorbed into your bloodstream, insuring your fluid balance. The feces then move through the colon to the rectum, the lower part of your intestine, and out of your body through the anus.

Problems with your digestive system can include: indigestion; disorders, diseases, and inflammation and infection of any of the digestive organs; appendicitis (inflammation of the appendix, which is a pouch at the point where the small and large intestine meet); inability to absorb nutrients; constipation (waste not leaving the body easily or often enough, causing the body to hold on to its toxins longer); food poisoning; hemorrhoids; hernia; jaundice; and diarrhea.

The Urinary System

Urine, a mixture of water and waste products, leaves your body as a by-product of a balanced system that also makes sure that your body retains the water and nutrients it needs for proper functioning.

Your kidneys, located at about waist level, behind your abdomen, filter waste from blood and facilitate the absorption into the bloodstream of chemicals you *do* need. These wastes are then mixed with water and salts in the kidneys to create urine. When you drink plenty of water, this helps dilute the waste products as they pass through your kidneys, thus reducing any negative effects these toxins may have on your body.

Urine then continues its journey out of each kidney, through tubes called ureters (one out of each kidney), and into the bladder, which is located in the center of the pelvic area. Toxic chemicals in your urine may concentrate in your bladder, which is another good reason to drink plenty of water—to flush out those toxins. Urine is stored in your bladder, and when the bladder is about half full, you'll begin to feel the urge to urinate. A sphincter muscle at the bladder's lower opening keeps the urine safely inside the bladder until you relax the muscle in order to urinate. At that point, the urine passes out of the bladder into the urethra, the tube that carries the urine to its final destination—the opening out of your body. The male urethra is eight inches long and runs through the penis. The female urethra is an inch and a half long and is entirely contained within the body.

Problems with your urinary system can include: inflammation, disorder, or disease of any of the system's components; changes in the nature of the urine; loss of bladder control (incontinence); and kidney stones.

The Endocrine System

*H*ormones are secreted by organs, and by cells of organs, and are carried by the bloodstream to tissues and other organs where they are required for the regulation of the particular functions of those organs and tissues.

Your endocrine system includes the glands that make those hormones, and the hormones themselves. The endocrine glands secrete hormones directly into your bloodstream. They are located throughout your body.

ADRENAL GLANDS. One adrenal gland sits above each kidney. The outer layer of the adrenals secrete the thirty-plus steroid hormones that regulate many processes, and the inner portion of the adrenals secrete epinephrine and norepinephrine, which change heart rate (increasing it and the force of its contractions), blood pressure, and available glucose sugar levels.

PANCREAS. Located behind the stomach, the pancreas creates insulin and glucagon, which maintain stable blood sugar levels. The pancreas also secretes nonhormonal chemicals, enzymes vital to the digestive process that break down sugars and starches, proteins and fats in the small intestine.

PITUITARY GLAND. Located just beneath the base of the brain between the two frontal lobes and behind the sphenoid sinus cavity, the pituitary controls all of the endocrine glands by receiving messages from throughout the body that call for particular hormones. Once the pituitary receives a call for a hormone, it then either secretes the hormone itself or secretes substances necessary for another gland to produce the hormone. The pituitary secretes somatotropin (a growth hormone); a thyroid-stimulating hormone, ACTH, which stimulates the adrenal glands; hormones required for the growth and release of sperm and egg cells; prolactin, which helps the mammary glands secrete milk; oxytocin, which is necessary for contractions during childbirth; and vasopressin, which helps the kidney maintain the proper water balance.

THYROID GLANDS. Located above the breastbone in front of the neck, the thyroid secretes hormones that regulate your metabolism. The four parathyroid glands are on the back and side of each lobe of the thyroid gland (the thyroid itself has two main lobes, one on either side of your windpipe, that are connected by tissue) and secrete parathyroid hormone, which regulates the level of calcium in your blood.

SEX GLANDS. The testes are the two male sex glands (also called the testicles), located behind the penis in the pouch known as the scrotum. The testes produce sperm and male sex hormones, such as testosterone, which perform many reproductive functions and control the male secondary sex characteristics (hair growth, penis size, sexual function, muscle mass, lower voice, and the like). The two ovaries are the female sex glands and are located in the pelvic area at the end of the fallopian tubes above and on either side of the uterus. The ovaries secrete the reproductive hormones estrogen and progesterone, which control ovulation (the monthly release of an ovary's egg), the menstrual cycle, and female secondary sex characteristics (such as breast development, hair growth, sexual function).

Problems in the endocrine system include: disorder, malfunction and disease of any of the system's components; hormone imbalance (which, in turn, causes a wide range of problems); diabetes; reproductive disorders.

The Nervous System

The star of the nervous system is the brain. During the 1980s, scientists and researchers learned more about the brain and central nervous system than in all prior human history. Prominent neuroscientist Dr. Deborah Mash calls the brain "the last biological frontier."

Your brain controls everything in your body by sending out to and receiving messages from the entire body. Different areas of your brain are responsible for controlling different aspects and functions of your body. The nervous system is the brain's link to all the sites in your body, and is comprised of neurons (nerve cells) that transmit these vital messages—which are chemical and electrical impulses—throughout the system. The chemicals that transmit impulses from one neuron to another (along the complex routes throughout your body) are called neurotransmitters.

The nervous system is divided into two integrated systems. The central nervous system is the central command center, and includes your brain, and the spinal cord, which extends from the base of the brain and acts as the path (protected by bones, tissue, and fluid) for the messages that the brain sends and receives.

The central nervous system links up to the peripheral nervous system, which carries these messages when they leave the central nervous system. The peripheral nervous system's components include the nerves that come out from the brain and the nerves that come out from the spinal cord. These nerves send and receive messages from receptor cells throughout the body. Within the peripheral nervous system is the autonomic nervous system, your automatic pilot in a very real sense: It regulates all of the involuntary actions of your body, which are all the functions of organs and systems that you do not voluntarily control. For instance, we don't say, "Now I'm going to have my liver detox my body." It's told to do it by the autonomic nervous system.

Within the brain is the cerebellum, which controls movement and balance; the thalamus, which controls various sensations including touch, pain, and temperature; the hypothalamus, which controls the body's involuntary processes and basic human desires; and the cerebral cortex, which has two sides, called hemispheres—the right hemisphere controls the left side of the body and the left hemisphere controls the right side.

Every action, every bodily function, every thought is regulated by *something* going on in your brain.

Problems with the nervous system include: both the physical and mental aspects of brain disorder, dysfunction, inflammation, and disease; and paralysis and other disorders of the spinal column.

The Reproductive System

Male

The male sex glands, called the testes (also referred to as testicles), produce the male sex hormone testosterone and sperm, the male reproductive cells that will ultimately travel out of the male's body to fertilize the female egg. The two testes are located in the scrotum, the sack behind the penis. Testosterone and other male hormones produced in other glands of the body control reproductive functions as well as the secondary male sex characteristics, which begin to appear at puberty.

Sperm travels through a number of ducts and passageways and mixes with fluid from the seminal vesicles, a thick, whitish substance secreted by the prostate gland, and some fluid from the urethra, which together make up the sperm-carrying liquid known as semen, which is expelled from the body by the penis. One sperm-carrying duct, the vas deferens, is snipped in the procedure known as vasectomy so that the sperm cannot make its way into the penis and only the carrier fluid, semen, will be ejaculated. The male's semen, now sperm-free, is consequently unable to fertilize a female's egg.

Problems in the male reproductive system include: dysfunction, disease, or inflammation of any of the system's components, which may also result in infertility and hormone imbalance and disorders stemming from such an imbalance; impotence; and, one of the most common problems for men over fifty, prostate inflammation, enlargement, or cancer.

Female

The female sex hormones estrogen and progesterone are produced by the two ovaries, the female sex glands. Estrogen regulates the menstrual cycle, preparing the uterus to receive a fertilized egg from the ovary by stimulating the uterine lining to grow. Progesterone declines after ovulation (the release of an egg by the ovary) if an egg hasn't been fertilized by sperm. If a woman doesn't become pregnant, the uterine lining is shed. This is a woman's monthly menstrual period.

The egg's journey begins in the ovary. It then passes through the fallopian tube into the uterus, where fertilization may occur when sperm passes up through the vagina, through the cervix, and into the uterus.

Fertilization occurs when the egg, released by the ovary just before or at the midpoint of a woman's monthly cycle, her most fertile time (the first day of a woman's period is considered day one; a cycle is on average about 28 days; so the midpoint is around day 14), is fertilized by a man's sperm. If the egg is fertilized it will then be implanted in the lining of the uterus and begin to grow. The growing, forming baby is called a fetus.

Approximately nine months after fertilization, the birth process begins. Uterine contractions propel the baby down through a dilated (widened) cervix, through the vagina (also called the birth canal), and out of the woman's body.

Problems in the female reproductive system include: dysfunction, disorder, and disease of its components; hormone imbalance and its resulting conditions; infertility; pregnancy, labor, and delivery difficulties and complications; and menstrual irregularities and difficulties.

NOTE: Breasts are also part of the reproductive system. They contain the mammary glands, which produce milk that is secreted from the breast's nipples, in order to feed the baby. Menopause is the cessation of the monthly menstrual cycle, and therefore fertility.

(Menopause is described in Part Three, in chapter IV, The Female Body, section 21.)

The Musculoskeletal System

Your bones and muscles work together with tendons and ligaments to form the musculoskeletal system. This amazing coordinated effort is responsible for all of your movements.

Most people don't realize that your bones are actually alive. Living tissue hardens to form bones, which not only form your body shape and protect internal organs but store 99 percent of your body's calcium, which is necessary to preserve the hardness and strength of each one of your 206 bones. Some bones have at their core marrow, which creates your body's red and white blood cells and platelets.

Your joints are the places where two or more bones meet. Joint movement is made possible by bands of tissue called ligaments, which are attached to the bones, and by elastic tissue called cartilage, which cover the ends of your bones. The ligaments connect your bones to each other, and the cartilage acts like a shock absorber, protecting and cushioning bones. Your joints contain fluid that helps with this process and also lubricates, for easy, painless movement.

The bones are attached to muscles by tissues called tendons. Your muscles are a very specialized kind of tissue that can contract. When muscles contract they tug on the tendons, which, because they're attached to your bones, make moving your body possible.

You have three types of muscles, each with specific design and function. Striated muscle looks almost like woven fabric and is attached to your skeletal structure, enabling your voluntary movements. Smooth muscle is found in many internal organs and large blood vessels and is part of functions that are involuntary. Smooth muscle is directly controlled by the autonomic nervous system. Cardiac muscle is the heart muscle, and it pumps blood within the heart and out from the heart. Like smooth muscle, cardiac muscle functions involuntarily and is controlled by the autonomic nervous system, but it is striated in form.

Bone disorders include: rheumatoid arthritis, systemic inflammatory disease of the joints that can gradually wear away cartilage, allowing the bones to rub together. Rheumatoid arthritis also affects other connective tissue and can progress to damage organs. Other bone disorders are bone fractures from injury; bursitis, an inflammation of joint fluid; hernia; lupus; osteoporosis; bone tissue deterioration; backache; slipped disk in the vertebrae; dislocated bones; tendonitis, an inflammation of the tendons; muscle strain, tears, and injury.

Skin

Your skin is one of the major organs of detoxification, because perspiration is one of the body's main waste and toxin elimination methods.

Even though there's no such thing as an average adult (although statistics, charts, and tables would like us to oversimplify and believe otherwise), science tells us that for an average adult, skin covers 18 square feet and weighs seven pounds. Keep in mind the difference between a five-foot tall, 90-pound adult and a six-foot-six-inch, 240-pound adult, and somewhere between those two adults lies the "average."

Your skin is waterproof, better than a rain slicker, and acts as a shield between the world and your body. Your skin also helps to regulate body temperature. It is composed of three layers: the thin outermost layer is the epidermis, followed by a much thicker dermis, and then a less thick subcutaneous layer.

The epidermis contains the pigment cells that determine your skin color and also helps protect against excessive sun exposure. The epidermis is quite hardy, and though it is continuously sloughing off, it also can repair and replace itself very quickly.

The dermis contains blood vessels, nerve endings, hair follicles, sweat glands, and oil glands. The blood vessels and the sweat glands help the body regulate heat. When you are hot, sweat secreted by the sweat glands flows through ducts to the surface of your skin where it evaporates, cooling the skin and also eliminating water, wastes, and toxins. The oil glands (sebaceous glands) coat the skin's surface with an oil called sebum, which helps prevent too much moisture from evaporating. When you wash your skin, you remove some of the sebum, causing a dry feeling, which is why your skin feels better after you've put on some moisturizing lotion.

The subcutaneous layer contains the bottom portion of the sweat glands, stored fat, blood vessels, and nerves.

The skin is also a sensory organ. The dermis and subcutaneous layer are filled with nerves and nerve endings that send touching and feeling signals to your brain.

When the skin's detoxing and other processes aren't working right, or there's interference by a foreign substance, the results can include: acne, fungal or bacterial infection, inflammation, blisters, corns, cysts, rashes, warts, moles, parasite infestation, lesions, disease, increased sensitivity to the sun, under-the-skin bleeding, and bruising.

Eyes

It sounds so simple, yet it's not: Light enters your eyes, where it is turned into impulses that your brain interprets as visual images.

Your eyeball is cradled in a socket, actually a cave of bone in your skull, and is cushioned by fat lining the socket. Tears released from glands located inside the upper eyelid moisten your eye and wash away debris. Your eyebrows, eyelashes, and eyelids work together to keep foreign substances out of your eyes.

Your eyeball consists of the sclera, the white of the eye; the cornea, the transparent, round part in the front; the iris, which is behind the cornea and has the pigment that gives your eyes their color; the pupil, the dark opening surrounded by the iris that can be small or large (dilated), depending on the level of light; and the lens, which is located behind the iris and focuses the light onto the retina, which are the special cells that line the back of the eye, thereby focusing your vision. Throughout the eye, various fluids nourish and assist in the eyes' functions.

Within the retina, cells called rods and cones perform the miraculous trick of converting light into electrical impulses, which are then transmitted by nerve endings to the brain through the optic nerve, which runs from the back of the eyeball directly to the brain.

And all *you* have to do to see is open your eyes.

Problems with your eyes include: distorted or diminished vision; inflammation, cataracts (a clouding of the lens); glaucoma (increased pressure within the eyeball due to faulty drainage); detached retina; deterioration, infection; and blindness.

Ears

Your ears translate sound vibrations into nerve impulses that the brain then interprets. This is the process that enables you to hear.

The outer ear receives sound waves through the ear canal to the eardrum. In the middle ear, these sound waves vibrate through three very small bones: the hammer, the anvil, and the stirrup. The vibrations then progress into the inner ear, where the spiral, seashell-shaped cochlea turns these vibrations into nerve impulses, which are in turn sent to the brain by way of the auditory nerve.

The ear is connected by the eustachian tube (located in the middle ear) to the upper part of your throat. It is this tube that is responsible for keeping the air pressure in the middle ear matched to the air pressure outside your body. This keeps the eardrum from rupturing, and it is why you will be advised not to fly on a plane if you have a cold, flu, or severe congestion in your head. The changes in cabin pressure can cause serious harm to your eardrum.

Passageways called the semicircular canals within the inner ear sense your head's motion and tell your brain. By doing so, these canals are responsible for maintaining your body's sense of balance (as in, not falling over, not getting dizzy, and not having motion sickness).

Problems with your ear can include: infection, partial or total deafness, pressure disorders in the inner ear, loss of balance, and eardrum damage.

The ears, nose, and throat are connected to one another by various passageways.

Nose

*A*s you'll recall from our tour of the respiratory system, your nose is one of the doors to the respiratory tract, and as such, it warms, moistens, and filters the air before it heads down your throat. Your nose hairs do the filtering, aided by mucus, which traps all foreign invaders, from dust to germs, and lubricates the nose and throat, thereby acting as a humidifier, too. Bacteria are killed either by chemicals in the mucus or by chemicals produced in the stomach, which kill the invaders that have managed to get past the nose and mouth and get swallowed.

Your sinuses are connected to your nose: four sets of them, located above, behind, and on either side of your nose. The sinuses are cavities filled with air—thus the sinus pain when the air pressure in these cavities differs from the air pressure outside your head. The sinuses are lined by glands that secrete mucus.

Your nose has another job as well, and that is to serve as a sensory organ for your sense of smell. When odors enter through your nostrils, nerve receptor cells transmit signals to your brain through the olfactory nerve. Smell can instantly trigger powerful memories and emotions, because the olfactory nerve takes a straight shot to the brain. Your sense of taste is also affected by your sense of smell. Taste is not only improved by smell, but can be temporarily impaired by it when congestion blocks your nose and reduces your ability to smell.

Problems with your nose may include: congestion; inflammation; infection; impaired sense of smell; nosebleeds; and in the sinuses, sinus pressure, congestion, and infection.

Throat

*Y*our throat is also called the pharynx. This passageway connects the back of the mouth and the nose to the esophagus, a long tube that runs down to your stomach. The pharynx also connects to the trachea, commonly referred to as the windpipe, the tube that goes to your lungs.

Your throat is part of both the respiratory and the digestive systems, and when all goes well, it sends air to the lungs and food to the stomach, not the other way around. Choking is what happens when food or an object gets lodged in your windpipe—in a very real sense, you've inhaled the object instead of swallowing it.

Your throat contains your tonsils, which are made up of lymphoid tissue. Tonsils are one of the first lines of defense, killing germs that enter your throat.

Your throat is five inches long and has three parts: upper, the nasopharynx, an open passage to your nose; middle, the oropharynx, which opens into your mouth; and lower, the laryngopharynx, which connects to the larynx, also known as the voice box, below it.

Your adenoids perform the same function as your tonsils and are located in the lining of the nasopharynx, on the way to the nose, and just above the tonsils (but you can't see them by looking into your throat).

Problems with your throat can include: dysfunction; inflammation or infection of any of the parts described above, or the tongue.

Teeth

Including wisdom teeth—which sometimes don't show up, and more often than not are removed when they do—an adult has thirty-two teeth. Your upper and lower jaws support your teeth, which make their home in your mouth.

Baby teeth, as they're commonly called, do not have the long talon-like roots that adult teeth have. When they fall out, they look pretty much as they did when they were in your mouth. Adult teeth, however, are a different story. Their roots snugly nestle into your gums, well below the gum line, reaching to the bone of the jaw.

The outer layer of a tooth is its enamel, which is usually a shade of white. Beneath the enamel is the dentin, whose yellowish color is the reason why teeth, as they age, become discolored if the enamel has worn thin or worn off.

Teeth are for biting, ripping, and chewing food. The front teeth on the top and bottom are the biters; the eye teeth, or bicuspids, next to them are essentially the rippers; and the molars in the back are the chewers. Your teeth are made of a similar substance as bone, and are therefore just as dependent on calcium for their strength and structural integrity.

Problems that can arise for the teeth and gums include: infection; inflammation; cavities (tooth decay); gum disease; cracked or loose teeth; bleeding gums; abscess near the tooth root or elsewhere; the death of the root, and therefore the tooth.

PART TWO

Natural Treatments

We're creating a new kind of family doctor, a doctor who blends the best of the diagnostic skills of the medical doctor with the more appropriate therapeutic skills of the naturopathic doctor, the Chinese Medical Doctor, and healers of other traditions.

—Joe Pizzorno, N.D.,
Doctor of Naturopathy, president
of Bastyr University

The Lord hath created medicines out of the earth; and he that is wise will not abhor them.

—Ecclesiastes 38:4

Introduction

*A*lternative medicine—it's the phrase on everyone's lips these days. Like the "overnight success" whose acting career was actually twenty years in the making, alternative medicine, which for centuries was the only medicine, has finally arrived, and is now welcome as an official branch of the modern mainstream medical family. Congress created the Office of Alternative Medicine (OAM) within the National Institutes of Health (NIH) in 1992, and it began accepting grant proposals early the following year. OAM's first-year budget was a miniscule $2 million out of the $10 billion total NIH budget, but by 1995 the OAM's budget had grown to $5.4 million. Still not much to work with, but it's an important beginning.

Ironically, it was the success of alternative medicine in saving the health, and possibly the life, of a politician that prompted the creation of the OAM. When retired Iowa Congressman Berkley Bedell was healed of both Lyme disease and prostate cancer by alternative medical treatments, he convinced Iowa Senator Tom Harkin to push for federally funded studies of alternative medicine. This new research branch, although not well funded, is at least a first step in what many enlightened physicians and consumers consider a new renaissance in medicine.

Among the many study areas that the OAM now funds, psychoneuroimmunology (PNI) is prominent. Science's technical term for the mind-body connection, PNI has always been central to holistic healing and alternative practices and is now mainstream medicine's hottest new field of research.

No longer the province of wholewheat hippies, vegetarians, Eastern philosophers, mystics, native peoples, and intellectuals, alternative medicine has burst out of the closet in America to a round of applause. Just plain folks numbering in the millions are no longer afraid someone will think they're wacky because they view their bodies holistically rather than just as individual parts, or because they supplement their mainstream medical care with herbal remedies, massage, acupuncture, meditation, or one of a host of other nonsurgical, nonpharmaceutical, preventive and healing natural treatments, practices, or foods.

There's nothing new about alternative medicine. It was the *original* medicine. What's new is that the mainstream medical and scientific community, after dragging its heels for the better part of the twentieth century, is finally giving alternative medicine due respect and deeming it worthy of further serious study. The motive is probably three-fold:

1. So much anecdotal evidence exists that alternatives work that the evidence simply can't be ignored or rationalized anymore.
2. The foundation has already been laid for much of the scientific study of alternative medicine.

   More than 25 percent of our mainstream pharmaceuticals are derived from plants, and 60 percent have additional plant-based ingredients. We already know the chemical properties of many other herbs and botanicals that heal or positively affect the body, mind, and spirit. These are used in natural treatments, but aren't yet being synthesized into pharmaceuticals. At least 20,000 scientific papers have been published in journals that attest to the efficacy of nutritional intervention regarding disease. In Europe, particularly Germany, scientists, medical researchers, physicians, and health practitioners are way, way ahead of the United States in this area.

   In the September 1995 issue of the journal *Alternative Therapies in Health and Medicine,* it's noted that as far as we've progressed, science still has a substantial amount of catching up to do: Of the 6,000 known medicinal herbs, only about 300 have been analyzed using modern scientific methods. The journal reports that some very high-profile independent organizations have begun programs to scientifically evaluate botanical products. The American Botanical Council (ABC), an Austin, Texas-based, nonprofit research and education association, is part of the largest single study of ginseng, "perhaps the most widely used herb on the market." The results will be published in *HerbalGram,* a quarterly journal published jointly by the ABC and the Herb Research Foundation (HRF).

The American Botanical Council is also bringing European expertise directly to American physicians, scientists, and consumers by translating and reviewing the 300 German Commission E monographs, "considered the most complete and accurate scientific information on herbs available worldwide." In 1976 the national health agency of Germany established Commission E to "oversee the efficacy and safety of herbal medicine." Made up of an expert panel of physicians, pharmacists, pharmacologists, toxicologists, and industry representatives, the commission independently evaluates scientific data on herbs and publishes the results as monographs in the *Federal Gazette.*

The Herb Research Foundation (HRF), which publishes *HerbalGram* jointly with the ABC, provides the only professional herb safety review service in the United States. The Boulder, Colorado-based nonprofit organization creates individual files from a search through available information in a library of more than 100,000 scientific articles, and so far have evaluated thirty individual herbs by a process that takes each herb's file through examination by an academic professional and a panel of scientific experts.

Within the natural health care industry, a number of groups are active as self-regulators, including the National Nutritional Foods Association (NNFA), which, among other educational and quality assurance programs, developed the "TruLabel" program to verify natural products through laboratory testing. Herbal companies that have enrolled in the program numbered 232 as of September 1995, accounting for 7,500 labels, *Alternative Therapies* reports.

The American Herbal Products Association (AHPA) is working on other programs, with the NNFA and on its own, having introduced a *List of Herbs of Commerce,* a pharmacopeia listing scientific names and properties of herbs. And the Association of Natural Medicine Pharmacists (ANMP) assists pharmacists by "providing accurate, thoroughly researched, and up-to-date information on the increasing variety of natural medicine."

3. Plain old economic panic is spurring interest in alternative medicine.

People *want* alternative medicine, and mainstream physicians are going to feel less change rattling around in their pockets if they continue to insist that theirs is the *only* way. Doctors know this, and in the spirit of "if you can't beat 'em, join 'em," are becoming aware of the great variety of health-promoting ways that can work in conjunction with, or in some cases, in place of drugs and surgery. These physicians can also feel more at ease now with alternative notions, thanks to the courage of those peers who have published best-selling books about their experiences in everything from nutrition therapies, meditation, Ayurvedic medicine, Chinese Medicine, and the mind-body connection to vitamin therapy, massage, and the body's spontaneous healing abilities.

None other than the prestigious *New England Journal of Medicine* paved the way for mainstream surge of interest in natural medicine back in January 1993, when they published "Unconventional Medicine in the United States—Prevalence, Costs, and Patterns of Use: Results of a National Survey."

The report, which made headlines across the country, stated that 33 percent of American adults (in the survey year 1990) had used alternative therapy to treat everything from headaches to cancer, spending an estimated $13.7 billion. The report shook up the mainstream medical community even further by revealing that those who sought out these treatments made more visits to alternative health care providers in a year than they did to *all* primary care mainstream physicians, and spent just as much money on alternative therapies as they spent out-of-pocket for *all* hospitalization expenses.

Most of these people—83 percent—used alternative treatment to supplement mainstream medical treatments. This next fact from the report may or may not come as a surprise: 72 percent of those surveyed used alternative treatments *without telling their mainstream physicians.*

Shortly after the appearance of this report, its author, Dr. David Eisenberg, an internist at Boston's Beth Israel Hospital and an instructor at Harvard Medical School, was the featured expert in "The Mystery of Chi," the first installment of Bill Moyers's critically acclaimed PBS series, *Healing and the Mind.* In this segment, Eisenberg, who in 1979 was the first medical exchange student sent by the National Academy of Sciences to the People's Republic of China, takes Moyers and his crew on a healing tour of China, exploring *chi,* the healing life energy accessed by its practitioners, and visiting among other places the Dongzhimen Hospital, where Eisenberg trained in the early 1980s.

Dongzhimen, one of the three traditional Chinese medical teaching hospitals in Beijing—"where Western and Chinese Medicine exist side by side," notes Eisenberg—has its own herbal pharmacy.

"Many of these herbs have been administered for thousands of years," Eisenberg reports, "and the effects have been documented and well studied."

In Moyers's companion book to the series, Eisenberg says he believes that Americans are "eager for a more complete way of seeing health," and indeed, the results of his *New England Journal of Medicine* report proved just that. Sensing that it's time mainstream physicians achieve balance in the practice of medicine by restoring natural practices to a system that has lost the essence of healing by relying overwhelmingly on hi-tech symptom-treating methods at the expense of natural preventive and healing methods that also focus on cause, changes are finally gripping our medical institutions.

"In a few years every hospital will have an alternative medicine section," predicts Deepak Chopra, M.D., best-selling author and director of the Chopra Center for Well-Being in LaJolla, California. "And every medical school will have an alternative department.

Medical students are *asking* for the exposure and the training. It's beginning."

Alternative treatment is simple common sense from any perspective. Treat the *cause*. And *prevent* it from happening again. Do it as *naturally* as possible.

These are three of the hallmarks of natural, or alternative, medicine, which also encompasses the holistic principle of treating the body, its mind, and spirit, as a whole.

Modern mainstream medicine is allopathic—synthetic, drug-oriented medicine—and it focuses on symptoms. Alternative medicine addresses the causes of illnesses, and uses substances and activities natural to the body, often from nature. Alternative medicine concentrates on wellness rather than illness, and it centers around the patient, not the doctor, emphasizing prevention and self-care. It focuses on naturally strengthening the body's systems, so the body can best release its own healing responses, something the body is exquisitely designed to do.

The line between mainstream and alternative health care is now dissolving. The two fields are on the verge of joining into one unified healing system that offers a variety of options. The two are also learning from each other. In the last few years, what was once considered alternative (even though it had plenty of scientific evidence to back it up) has become accepted by the drug-and-surgery-oriented mainstream medical establishment. The roles of nutrition (foods, herbs, vitamins, minerals), prevention, state of mind, and environmental factors have finally been recognized as crucial to good health and healing. Studies are now under way that will enable researchers to understand certain elusive healing mechanisms, including those we haven't yet figured out how to measure in the lab, such as healing energies, or *chi* in the Chinese medical tradition. In the early 1990s, scientists and doctors at New York University began looking into ways of measuring these energies in the body and in the bodies of those who can sense and direct this energy, such as Chinese healers.

Studies have shown that the higher a person's education and income, the more likely they are to seek alternative treatments. But that is changing, too. As alternative, natural approaches have become more publicized, people of every educational and economic level are becoming active in their own health care. They seek out information, which is now even easier to find. It's as close as your nearest bookstore, personal computer, or the health report on your local nightly news.

In *Dr. Braly's Food Allergy and Nutrition Revolution,* Dr. James Braly takes a strong stand, as do many other physicians who have embraced natural medicine: "The single greatest barrier in medicine today is the government regulations that prevent most alternative medicines from promoting their ability to treat and reverse disease," he notes. "Herbs and vitamins, for example, can't be marketed with medicinal claims. This healing information *is* getting to people, but very slowly and only to people who search for it. Alternative medicine should be able to make claims as long as they've got the science and facts to back them up. Otherwise, we end up institutionalizing *bad* medicine, which is what's happened. One out of seven people in the hospital today are there because of the bad effects of FDA *approved* drugs."

Our bodies are designed to produce and release their own healing chemicals that are highly responsive to every situation.

"We know that the chemical makeup of tears of joy is different than tears of sadness, for example," Dr. Deepak Chopra says. Chopra is a pioneer in modern Ayurvedic medicine, which grew out of the traditional medicine of his native India. Ayurveda literally means "science of life," and the mind-body connection is crucial to this healing system, which emphasizes the proper foods, herbs, environment, exercise, and specific healing practices for your body and personality type, as well as meditation, massage, and aligning the body, mind, and consciousness in order to trigger our natural healing response.

The chemicals in our bodies, Chopra explains, are part of an internal pharmacy of naturally created painkillers, antibiotics, tranquilizers, stimulants, and even anti-cancer medicines that are produced inside us exactly when and where they are needed. What all of the alternative, natural practices and treatments have in common is their focus on and ability to help our bodies heal themselves. The mind is an integral part of the process. "Expectation influences outcome," is the phrase usually applied to this phenomenon.

The mind-body connection is at the root of Native American medicine, too. Raised with its traditions as well as twentieth-century's advanced technology and education, psychologist Brooke Medicine Eagle is a teacher of natural ways, an Earthkeeper, and author of *Buffalo Woman Comes Singing*, a moving account of Native American wisdom and healing in practice, which has quickly become a classic in the field. Brooke recalls what motivated her to explore her healing heritage more than twenty-five years ago: "I began to understand what was missing. The wholeness of the person wasn't being addressed (in Western medicine and culture). So I began to look at my own people's work in body, mind, spirit, and emotions. Western medicine covers the body, but in order to *heal*, you need to look at a much larger level. People are turning to alternative medicine because mainstream isn't working entirely. That's because it only concerns itself with symptoms. So, people look around for something else."

Her work is spiritual and psychological. "The psychology of our experiences is no longer distinct from our physical healing. I live by the motto, 'Embodying spirit.' We are whole and we are holy. It's not that we don't know these deep truths, it's that we haven't embraced them in our bodies and daily ways of living."

She believes that non-Native Americans who are now studying and embracing these traditional philosophies and practices are doing so because "they work. Being in harmony with all things is an eternal truth, not just a Native American truth." Plenty of folks fill lecture halls to hear Brooke Medicine Eagle speak and join her for specialized retreats where they not only learn about but experience the essence of living the body-mind-spirit connection through movement, music, meditation, visual interpretation, herbs, and spiritual experiences.

Kevin Ryerson, another modern-day spiritual explorer, has worked closely with biomedical researchers as an expert intuitive. An associate of the pioneering Center for Applied Intuition near San Francisco, Ryerson was a major contributor to Jason Serinus's *Psy-*

choimmunity: Key to the Healing Process, and Dr. Gabriel Cousen's *Spiritual Nutrition.* Both books focus on the relationship between spirituality and health.

"A staple of holistic healing is prevention, and now that's the core issue of the health crisis in the country," says Ryerson, who has been working on new research with Dr. Cousens in healing herbs, plants, and food sources indigenous, rather than introduced, to the particular environment. "The triumph of holistic thinking is balance, and the holistic philosophy is transforming our major institutions."

Searching for anti-cancer chemicals in nature, the natural products branch of the National Cancer Institute collects marine organisms and botanicals from around the world, placing major emphasis on plants from the rain forest. That's because "rain forests are the lungs of the planet," Ryerson remarks, "and the planet's apothecary."

Scientists and physicians are aware of medicine's impending transformational shift, as mainstream and alternative medicine join hands. When the government and medical establishment lend their support, something that was considered alternative or unorthodox on Monday will be welcomed with open arms on Tuesday.

Acupuncture and Acupressure

Integral to the practice of Chinese Medicine, these ancient, proven vibrational medicine techniques of acupuncture and acupressure correct imbalances, clear blockages, and realign your body's life force energy, which the Chinese call *chi,* by inserting very fine (and painless) needles into or applying pressure on specific points along your body's energy pathways, which are called meridian lines.

Both of these techniques are now routinely recommended by mainstream physicians because of their excellent results in the prevention and treatment of a wide variety of physical and emotional conditions. The professional organizations listed in the Resources section at the end of the book can recommend certified practitioners in your area, or you may ask your physician for a referral. Certified acupuncture and acupressure practitioners can now be found in virtually every community in the nation. Some of these practitioners are also naturopathic physicians, chiropractors, and nutritionists. Sometimes they practice other forms of healing as well.

Acupuncture is also used in surgical procedures as an alternative to anesthesia. The patient feels no pain and remains alert, but relaxed. This is ideal for those who suffer from allergic or other adverse reactions to anesthetics.

Ayurveda

The ancient medical tradition of India, Ayurveda literally means "science of life," and treats the body, mind, and spirit as a unified whole. All treatments and practices have at their core the Ayurvedic system of the three *doshas*—mind-body types—Vata, Pitta, and Kapha. Each of us have some of the traits and components of each of the doshas, but we usually fit more into one category than another. Vatas, the thinnest of the three mind-body types, tend to move quickly and grasp new information quickly. Their mental and physical energy comes in bursts. Vatas are prone to worry, irregular hunger, and digestion, are enthusiastic, imaginative, excitable, and have a tendency to overexert themselves. Vata is associated with your body's movement, and its major function is to control your central nervous system. Bringing Vata qualities into balance in any body type brings the other doshas into balance almost automatically.

Pittas are of medium build, have fair, ruddy, or freckled skin, have difficulty tolerating hot weather, can become irritable when under stress, like challenges, have a sharp intellect and articulate speech, strong digestion and a healthy appetite, are well proportioned with medium strength and endurance, and are outspoken, orderly, and efficient. Pitta controls metabolism in all the mind-body types. In his book *Perfect Health*, Deepak Chopra, M.D., reminds us that "Every cell in the body relies on Pitta dosha to regulate its intake of pure food, water, and air. Toxins of all types show up quickly as Pitta imbalance"—no matter what your mind-body type or combination of types. Those with an abundance of Pitta characteristics, then, are particularly sensitive to *all* toxins, and especially to toxic emotions.

Kaphas are the heaviest, sturdiest, and most relaxed of the three mind-body types. Kaphas have steady energy, physical strength, and endurance, move slowly, have a tendency to be overweight, are slow to anger, have slow digestion and sleep longer, are slow to take in new information but have excellent memories, are affectionate, open-minded, possessive, empathic, and take a long time to make decisions. Kapha controls the body's moist tissues and "gives us a sense of inner security and steadiness, an essential aspect of a healthy person," notes Dr. Chopra.

The three doshas essentially show who you are and how you interact with your environment. The goal is to balance the doshas via nutrition, meditation, herbs, yoga, breathing, exercise, detoxification, bodycare, rest, and changes in your routine and environment. Specific physical, emotional, and spiritual symptoms signal us that a dosha is out of balance. Even though we may have the characteristics of one particular dosha over the other two, there are aspects of all three within every person.

Bodywork

Any method used to manipulate, massage, knead, or stretch the soft tissue, muscles, and joints is termed bodywork. Bodywork includes massage, deep tissue massage, neuromuscular massage, lymphatic drainage massage, shiatsu, reflexology, rolfing, osteopathic medicine, chiropractic medicine, yoga, touch therapies, and movement therapies such as the Feldenkreis Method and Alexander Technique, as well as many other treatments. Some focus on particular parts of your body, such as reflexology, which uses foot massage to trigger the body's healing mechanisms, or lymphatic drainage massage, which focuses on your lymph glands. Other treatments can be used on the entire body. Research has shown that bodywork treatments strengthen your body's immune system, enabling you to resist and combat disease, improve circulation, restore proper muscle function and range of movement, relieve fluid congestion, relieve pain, and restore well-being by triggering mood-enhancing brain chemicals.

Chinese Medicine

A comprehensive medical system dating back to ancient times, Chinese Medicine uses herbal preparations, acupressure, acupuncture, hands-on energy healing, and other natural methods to treat the body, mind, and spirit, which are viewed as a unified whole. The goal is to stimulate the body's defenses and healing mechanisms so that the body is better able to perform its natural function of healing itself. Historically, a doctor in China was considered a good doctor based upon how many of his patients were *well*. Causes are of primary importance and symptoms are viewed to be what they really are: expressions of an underlying problem that needs to be addressed. The healing system operates all the time and can diagnose, repair, and neutralize. Another principle of Chinese Medicine is the belief that healing can also be triggered and aided by the mind or slowed down and prevented by the mind. The placebo effect is an excellent example of the mind-body connection since it is literally the ability of the mind that heals, without any outside chemical intervention.

In Chinese Medicine, the attitude of the doctor or other health care practitioner is extremely important. "The doctor's mind should be one with the mind of the patient. The doctor also has to *be* the patient," is the guiding principle of ancient Chinese teachings regarding medicine.

Chinese Medicine includes an elaborate understanding of the workings of *chi*, your body's life-force energy, throughout the body, mind, and spirit. Literally everything in your life and environment affects this vital life force. The Chinese healing arts also include detoxification, moxibustion (the use of heat on specific points of the body), yoga, meditation, breathing techniques, and movement techniques such as Tai Chi and Chi Gong.

Essential Oils and Aromatherapy

Concentrated natural oils and essences of trees, herbs, shrubs, grasses, plants, flowers, and fruits are used externally for their medicinal properties as antiseptics, antibiotics, antivirals, and antifungals. The essential oils of many botanicals are often twice, ten times, or even twenty-five times more powerful than the synthetic chemicals found in manufactured products and drugs. When used on the skin and absorbed into your body through the skin, essential oils do not accumulate but are eliminated through the body's natural processes between three and fourteen hours afterward, depending upon your size and state of health. Essential oils stimulate the body's systems and healing mechanisms, and whether used on a surface, the body, or diffused in the air each has one or more of the following properties: antiseptic, antiviral, antibacterial, antifungal, antiinflammatory, antineuralgic, antirheumatic, antispasmodic, analgesic, antidepressant, hypotensol, hypertensol, deodorizing, sedative, diuretic.

Used also in aromatherapy for the added effects of their fragrances, essential oils are just as powerful. Our sense of smell has direct access to the limbic system of the brain, the seat of our emotions. When an oil is diffused in the air, it can have a profound effect on our state of emotional well-being.

Look for the words *Pure Essential Oil* on all bottles of essential oils. Only pure, natural essential oils will have all their medicinal properties intact. An "oil compound" or an "aroma" is *not* a pure essential oil. To see if a product is the real thing, blot it on a piece of paper. Ironically, pure essential oils will not leave an oily mark. The fakes will.

Essential oils are not all priced the same, which will be another indication of whether or not you are buying a pure essential oil. Their market value is determined by the cultivation and production costs of each individual botanical, including transportation from its country of cultivation. For example, the Purple Isle Aromatherapy catalog lists (as I write this) a 5 ml bottle of cinnamon essential oil at

$30.40, while the same-size bottle of lavender essential oil retails for only $9.30. Essential oils are sold in dark-colored glass bottles. Keep them in those bottles, tightly closed. Store the bottled oils away from light, heat, and humidity. These measures are taken to protect their potency. Many treatments call for a blend of particular pure essential oils because each individual oil can enhance the therapeutic effects of another.

Studies show the power of using essential oils for their disease-fighting, purifying, and healing properties. Studies also reveal their powerful effects when used in aromatherapy. Beta brain waves, present in our ordinary state of awareness, are increased when the aroma of stimulating oils like rosemary or basil are inhaled. Calming oils, such as jasmine, lavender, and rose, produce more alpha and theta brain waves, which cause our slower, more relaxed, meditative states, the very states linked to your body's healing abilities.

Herbs and Botanicals

The use of herbs and botanicals, discussed extensively throughout this book, has its roots (pun intended) in every culture's medical practices. What grows from the ground or in water (marine botanicals) is given to us by nature for therapeutic use, as well as nourishment and the care of the body, mind, and spirit. Most of the herbs and botanicals we use fall into the category of Western herbs (those cultivated originally outside the Orient) or Chinese herbs (cultivated originally only in the Orient, but now also grown in the West). Historically, Western herbs were used in the West, and Chinese herbs in the Orient. Now, however, all are available for cultivation and purchase across the globe.

When you buy herbs or botanicals, you'll want to use only tinctures (liquids, usually in small bottles with droppers built in to their caps or lids), or capsules that expressly state on the label that they have been made with freeze-dried extracts. Why? Because tinctures and freeze-dried extracts in capsules have been prepared in ways that prevent them from losing their potency and effectiveness. Many teas, depending upon ingredients, preparation, and place of purchase, can be as effective as tinctures and freeze-dried extract in capsules. This is especially true of those already potent botanicals that are marketed for their medicinal use, or those that can cause side effects. Herbal preparations provided by a Chinese Medical Doctor are also very potent. One of the exceptions to this rule is echinacea, which is only really effective, given current preparation, storage, and marketing methods, when used as a tincture or freeze-dried extract capsule. Echinacea, derived from the root, stem, and leaves of the purple coneflower, is a proven and safe immune system-boosting herb. It is discussed frequently throughout this book.

Herbs and botanicals must be handled with as much care, caution, and respect as anything else you put into your body. Just because something is natural does not mean that it is always safe for everyone under all circumstances. Pay special attention to the sections in this book that discuss the proper use of herbs and the side effects and dangers of some herbs and botanicals.

Native American and Native Peoples' Medicine

*B*ased entirely on the principles of nature and the unification of body, mind, and spirit, the medicine of Native Americans and other native peoples across the globe is, of course, our very first medicine. It survives to this day, already validated by modern science in many areas, including the use of herbs and botanicals, the effects of the mind on the body, the importance of nutrition, detoxification, and keeping to the guiding principles of nature. The term *medicine,* in the Native American tradition, refers not only to medical healing but to life's many lessons, which are, of course, also healing experiences. Often you'll hear about the medicine and teachings of animals, the earth, the wind, water, and other elements of nature when studying or using Native American healing methods and philosophy. For example, the "medicine" of the mouse, as Jamie Sams and David Carson recount in their book *Medicine Cards: The Discovery of Power Through the Ways of Animals,* is scrutiny. If you see a mouse, rather than just screaming "Eeek!" learn from its message. And the message of scrutiny is: "It is good medicine to see up close. It is good medicine to pay attention to detail, but it is bad medicine to chew every little thing to pieces." Another one of the mouse's messages is that "there is always more to learn."

The medicine of the squirrel is gathering: "It teaches you how to gather and store your energy for times of need. It teaches you to reserve something for future use, whether it be a judgment, an opinion, a savings account, candles, or extra food." Squirrel medicine tells us to be ready for change by letting go of "things that do not serve you." The squirrel brings us a clear message about detoxing: Know when to gather, and know when to release.

While each culture may have its own specific rituals, traditions, and terminology, their foundations in the power of nature and our own bodies to heal is identical. India's Ayurveda, Chinese Medicine, the Hawaiian healing tradition of Huna, and Native American medicine all operate, for example, on the premise that each of us has a blueprint for perfect health in our bodies, and therefore in our minds and spirits as well, and it is this blueprint that enables us to heal, or even spontaneously heal. Spiritual beliefs are woven into the healing traditions of all native peoples, just as our spirits are one with our minds and our bodies.

Nutrition and Vitamins

Since absorbing nutrients into our bloodstream is essential to supporting life, proper nutrition and proper nutrient absorption (including the use of vitamins and other supplements) is vital to our health and our very survival, and is discussed extensively throughout this book. The role that nutrients play in preventing disease and healing is an essential one, but like everything else about you, balance is the key. More is not always better, and mega-doses of vitamins and nutrients in some instances can be toxic. You'll find a thorough discussion of this aspect in Part Three, chapter V, number 25, in the section on vitamins.

Research continues to show how nutrients play very specific roles within our bodies, and how simply changing the way we eat can lead to better health and healing. Some of what we eat, though, can be toxic, and you'll find an extensive discussion of this in Part Three, in chapter V, Food.

Vibrational Medicine

We are energy in a literal sense. Chemical and electrical energy surges throughout our bodies constantly. It's what keeps us alive and functioning properly. We are affected by our internal energy and the energy that radiates from our bodies (our energy field), as well as the energy outside our body system that can either interfere with our health (for example, radiation poisoning, which is caused when radiation is delivered in excess to the body via direct contact with something radioactive or via the direct contact with an x ray, a beam of radioactive energy) or it can enhance our health.

Healing with energy is called vibrational medicine, because all energy vibrates. Yes, even ours. And the interactions between the vibrational frequencies of our bodies and the external energies we use therapeutically can cause many changes in our body and mind, inducing healing. Vibrational medicine includes:

LIGHT THERAPY. The use of full-spectrum light, individual components of the spectrum, and colors or colored light to detoxify, normalize, and heal.

MUSIC AND SOUND THERAPY. The use of sound waves to heal the body, mind, and spirit.

HOMEOPATHY. The use of minute, greatly diluted, essences of a substance to promote healing. These essences are the same ones that could make you ill if you were well, but ironically, if you are ill, they help to heal. Homeopathy is both a botanical and a vibrational medicine, since it works on the level of the natural ingredients and on a subtle energy level because such a small amount of the ingredient is used.

ACUPUNCTURE AND ACUPRESSURE. The use of fine needles or external pressure on specific points along your body's energy pathways (meridian lines) to correct imbalances, clear blockages in your body's energy flow, and realign your body's life force energy, thus leading to healing. These are classified as Vibrational Medicine because they interact with and manipulate the body's own internal energy via energy pathways and the specific points along them.

HANDS-ON ENERGY HEALING. Also called "Energy Field Work," its practitioners can sense and redirect energy within your body, leading to balance and healing. Mainstream medicine regularly practices a version of this called therapeutic touch, which is routinely offered in hospitals and healthcare facilities across the country.

BODYWORK, MASSAGE, AND MOVEMENT THERAPIES. The use of these methods extends into your internal energy as well as external energy fields. These therapies are enhanced by the energy interaction between you and the practitioner and by the realignment, clearing, and revitalization of your life-force, electrical, and chemical energies that take place during any hands-on treatment.

THE BACH FLOWER REMEDIES. Like other methods that use the essence of something organic, such as homeopathy, these remedies operate according to the principle of cellular memory and the ability of an essence's energy vibration to heal even when that essence is present only in a minute amount.

These Vibrational treatments, as well as the vibrational modalities of healing with the natural energies of water, crystals, minerals, electromagnetic fields, and the effects of one person's energy upon another's are part of the fastest-growing area of study in science and medicine today.

PART THREE

50 Toxic Situations, Preventions, and Antidotes

There are so many unseen negative influences on human health that are missed by conventional medical practitioners that many sources of human suffering remain undetected.

—Richard Gerber, M.D.,
Vibrational Medicine

Western medical researchers are just beginning to realize the ancient masters understood profound aspects of the human mind and body without the aid of sophisticated diagnostic machines.

—Stephen Pan, Ph.D.,
Director, East Asian Research Institute,
New York City

Your remedies shall be your food, and your food shall be your remedies.

—Hippocrates

All-Purpose Antidotes

The All-Purpose Antidotes that follow can often be used as preventives and antidotes in each of the fifty situations.

Throughout the situations described in Part Three, I will advise you when to use the All-Purpose Antidotes and which of them are most beneficial to the situation.

I will also advise you when *not* to use a specific All-Purpose Antidote if it may be harmful to a particular physical condition, such as pregnancy, or if it may interact with medications you may be taking.

1. *Eight glasses of pure bottled (or home-filtered) water daily* to flush out the toxins and waste in your systems, to provide water balance, and to rehydrate.
2. *Fiber in your diet* from foods including organic vegetables, fruits, and grains. The amount of fiber varies with each person's system and sensitivities. If you eat a balanced diet of organic, nonprocessed fruits, vegetables, and grains and move your bowels (without constipation) at least once each day—or up to three times, if you are a large person with a higher food intake—then you probably have adequate fiber in your diet.
3. *The herb echinacea* to boost your immune system, prevent and treat illness, and promote healing. (See chapter VI, Illness, Injury, and Healing, section 31, *In the Spotlight:* Cold and Flu, for a thorough description and dosage information.)

4. *The antioxidant vitamins* C, E, and beta carotene to strengthen your systems, prevent illness, encourage absorption of vital nutrients, and promote healthy detoxification.

5. *Dandelion root* in tea, capsules, or other forms to gently and effectively detox your liver and every cell in your body. Nontoxic, it can be taken regularly. Standard dose: one capsule in the morning and one in the early evening by 6 P.M. If taken later than that you may wake up in the middle of the night to urinate. Dandelion root is a must if you stress your liver in any way, including drinking alcohol.

6. *Meditation and relaxation techniques and experiences,* including yoga and breathwork.

7. *Daily exercise in any form,* including sports, walking, stretching, workouts, yoga, dance, and movement.

8. *Oriental detoxifying teas,* such as Oriental Black Soybean Tea, made by boiling eight dried black soybeans in 4½ cups of pure spring water in a nonmetal pot. When the liquid is reduced by half, add a pinch of sea salt and simmer for two minutes; strain and drink one cup per day as needed. This tea purifies the blood, eliminates toxins, clears the skin, and relaxes.

   Oriental Radish Tea is made by putting two tablespoons of grated raw daikon radish and a pinch of sea salt into one cup of pure bottled or home-filtered water; boil for one to two minutes. Let tea cool a bit. Drink once a day as needed. This well-known Japanese purifying and detoxing tea works well against all toxins and if you've overindulged in rich foods.

9. *Bodywork of any kind, massage, and yoga postures,* all of which stimulate your systems and detoxification processes.

10. *Lymphatic drainage massage* to clear the lymph system of stagnant, blocked, sluggish fluid. This fluid carries toxins toward eventual release by the body.

11. *Detox skin* by sloughing off dead cells with non-toxic alpha-hydroxy organic acids (often referred to as fruit acids) found in foods, particular citrus and other fruits. Use the inside of a lemon, lime, or papaya peel to gently smooth over your skin in the evening before bed, or buy nontoxic, organic alpha-hydroxy acid preparations in health food stores. These preparations may also include other natural alpha-hydroxy acids, such as lactic acid (found in sour milk) and tannic acid (found in red wine). Although they can irritate sensitive skin if used in too high a concentration or too often, these preparations are good for reducing wrinkles and fine lines, treating acne, exfoliation, and toning, all of which promote detoxification through the skin. Do not use synthetic chemical fruit acids found in many over-the-counter products sold in pharmacies and higher-priced lines of beauty products.

Detox your face with natural cleansers. This helps release internal toxins as well as the external ones of dirt and pollution that lodge on the skin and in the pores. Apricot kernel and almond scrubs remove dead cells and unclog pores. Clay masks draw out toxins, remove dead cells, tighten pores, loosen blackheads, as well as improve circulation and lymphatic drainage. Use pure aloe gel on blemishes to heal, dry out, detoxify, and smooth without scarring. For acne scars or other scarring, gently rub in pure vitamin E oil every night. Aloe will also heal burns, cuts, abrasions, and sunburn.

12. *Detox hair* by getting rid of the buildup from hair care products. Mix one tablespoon brown rice vinegar with one cup warm water and use as a final rinse after shampooing, before conditioning.

13. *Essential oils* that detoxify and can be used in the air with diffusers, lamp rings, in the wax of a melting candle; on surfaces as a cleaner/detoxifier; or on your

body by adding them to the bath or massage lotion, include the following, which are each antibacterial, antiviral, antiseptic, and antifungal oils: eucalyptus lemon, eucalyptus radiata, lavender, tea tree, and thyme. Cinnamon, clove, and ravensara perform all of the above "anti" functions except fungal. So does garlic, but you probably won't want to put garlic on your body but *in* it, and use it as a surface cleaner/detoxifier in the home, workplace or any other location. Other essential oils have a variety of "anti" properties and many are noted within the preventives and antidotes in Part Three.

14. *Vibrational Medicine* includes acupressure, acupuncture, music/sound in healing, light therapy, Bach Flower Remedies, therapeutic touch or hands-on energy healing, all powerful tools of detoxification that clear, repair, realign, balance all of our energies and energy fields. Seek the assistance of a reputable (often certified, depending upon the therapeutic area) healing professional.

I

Addictions and Habits

1. Caffeine

Found in coffee, tea, chocolate, cocoa, soft drinks, and as an ingredient in more than 2,000 nonprescription drugs. A stimulant, caffeine in small to moderate doses promotes alertness and elevates mood, but in large doses it overstimulates, causing jitters, irritability, insomnia, heart palpitations, and accelerated heartbeat. It can also cause more serious heart, circulation, neurological, and digestive problems for those who already have impairment or illness in those areas and for those who are sensitive to caffeine's stimulating effects.

Prevention

Many people are addicted to caffeine and don't realize it. Sure signs of your body's addiction are withdrawal symptoms: headache, difficulties concentrating, tiredness, and irritability when you skip caffeine for a day or cut back on it. To prevent caffeine's toxic and habit-forming effects, cut back gradually or cut out caffeine entirely, switch to decaffeinated products, blend decaffeinated with caffeinated, or switch to beverages with lower caffeine content (for instance, colas are much lower in caffeine than coffee).

Antidotes

To detox from caffeine's effects, rehydrate and flush out your system by drinking daily at least eight glasses of pure water, which will also help counteract caffeine's dehydrating, diuretic effect. Also, use any or all of the All-Purpose Antidotes.

CAFFEINE CONTENT IN BEVERAGES AND CHOCOLATE

Drip or percolated coffee (one cup)	115–180 mg.
Brewed coffee (one cup)	80–135 mg.
Instant coffee (one cup)	65–100 mg.
Tea (one cup)	30–50 mg.
Coca-Cola (12 oz.)	46 mg.
Pepsi (12 oz.)	38 mg.
Chocolate (one oz.)	6–26 mg.*

NOTE: Milligrams vary depending upon the strength of the coffee or tea and how much you use—that is, how strong a brew you make—to prepare one cup of liquid.

*Milligrams vary depending upon type and quality of the chocolate. Dark or bittersweet pure chocolate is higher in caffeine content than milk chocolate.

2. Food

For all food habits and addictions, including sugar, see chapter V, Food.

3. Nicotine

Found only in the tobacco plant, nicotine is the active addictive substance in cigarettes, cigars, pipe tobacco, and chewing tobacco. It is commonly delivered into the body's systems through smoking (inhaling or just puffing) or chewing. Nicotine is a stimulant with a powerful effect on the nervous system. Nicotine and the many other chemicals in tobacco and its smoke, including tar, have been linked to cancer, respiratory diseases, circulatory disorders, immune system suppression, and many other conditions resulting from tobacco's effects on the organs and biochemical processes of the body.

Prevention

The obvious preventive is not to use nicotine products or, at the very least, cut way back on their use. To help prevent some of the toxic effects of nicotine use, increase your daily intake of vitamin C, as this vitamin in particular is depleted by smoking. Ester-C, a form of vitamin C that is better absorbed by the body and doesn't have any acidic side effects in your stomach, is recommended. Also, be sure to take the other antioxidants, vitamin E and beta carotene in the following doses: 2,000 mg. Ester C and 400 I.U. vitamin E daily; every other day take 25,000 I.U. beta carotene. Overdoing vitamin E and beta carotene can make you feel sluggish and cause muscle weakness. So, unless you've got a diagnosed severe depletion of these nutrients, stick with the above formula. You may increase your dosage of vitamin C if needed; your body will quickly eliminate what it doesn't need, which you'll notice by an increase in urination and a light lemon-colored urine.

Antidotes

If you're smoking or chewing tobacco, you're ingesting toxins with each puff or chew. The antioxidants described above are also a detox treatment. The most important part of your treatment is regular use of the All-Purpose Antidotes, with particular emphasis on the use of echinacea, dandelion root, water, and bodywork.

4. Alcohol

Primarily ingested in beverages such as hard liquor, wine, beer, and liqueurs, alcohol is also found in small amounts in over-the-counter and prescription products such as mouthwash and cough syrup, and as a preservative in natural flavorings and herbal liquids. Alcohol is physiologically a depressant but can produce a diverse range of re-actions, from giddiness, euphoria, and boisterous behavior to nas-tiness, rage, and despair. Alcohol can make you sleepy, too much can make you pass out, more than too much can result in fatal alcohol poisoning.

Alcohol is processed by the liver, and excessive alcohol con-sumption results in extreme toxicity and diseases of the liver, in-cluding cancer and cirrhosis. It takes the liver one hour to break down the alcohol in one average drink. Researchers at the UCLA Medical Center report that when a liver is diseased (as happens after long-term frequent alcohol consumption), it releases toxins into the bloodstream that travel to the brain and may trigger bouts of irri-tability, anger, rage, disorientation, anxiety, and apathy, which may explain the behavioral outbursts associated with alcoholism.

Prevention

Before drinking alcohol, drink a couple of glasses of water. This will slow down your body's absorption of the alcohol. Do not drink on an empty stomach. While these and other precautions are helpful for light social drinkers, heavier, regular consumption of alcohol and al-coholism are ongoing toxic conditions and must be treated profes-sionally.

Antidotes

For light to moderate social drinking, the following treatments help detox from the physical effects of alcohol. They can also be used to help detox heavy drinkers and alcoholics, combined with a profes-sional treatment program.

AFTER DRINKING: If it's in the evening, before going to bed take 1,000 mg. of vitamin C (the Ester C form) and drink two 8 oz. glasses of pure water. Between the time you drink the water and uri-nating, however, the toxins in your body will be released, which will make you feel a bit inebriated again. If you have not urinated within fifteen minutes after drinking the water, drink another glass. After urinating, go to sleep. If you are drinking during the day, follow the same process without the sleeping, unless you feel like taking a nap. Drinking coffee in an attempt to sober up will only make you into what's been called a "wide-awake drunk." Coffee is a diuretic, like alcohol, and will further dehydrate you, when what you really need is to rehydrate and flush out the alcohol toxins with water.

EACH DAY YOU CONSUME ALCOHOL: Drink two cups of dandelion root tea, one in the morning and one in the evening, or take two dandelion root pills each day, one in the morning and one in the evening, to detox your liver. If you drink on a regular basis, take the dandelion pills even on the days you do not consume alcohol. The herb milk thistle *(Silybum marianum)* is also an effective antidote to alcohol, as it stimulates the regeneration of liver cells and protects them from toxins. Take two capsules in the morning and two capsules in the evening on the day you drink and the day after. If you are a regular drinker, take the capsules every day, even on days you do not consume alcohol. Also, use the All-Purpose Antidotes, with emphasis on bodywork and lymphatic drainage massage to flush the toxins from your body.

5. Over-the-Counter, Prescription,

and Illegal Drugs

See section 26, Medications, in chapter VI, Illness, Injury, and Healing.

In the Spotlight

6. Alcohol and Drug Addiction

Those who are chemically addicted to both alcohol and drugs have so severely compromised their health that they are walking toxic-waste dumps.

Treatment programs approach addiction from the physical, psychological, and spiritual angles, and treatment professionals know that one approach will not work without the other two. Before we get into some of the specifics of the natural approaches to detoxing the addicted body, mind, and spirit, let's look at some of the components of overall addiction treatment.

Every good treatment center creates an individualized treatment plan based on the person's needs. The majority of centers also include A.A. and other 12-step programs in their treatments because they're a proven form of recovery and aftercare for many addicted people. These 12-step programs have spirituality at their core. In fact, the first mainstream medical community embrace of the spiritual component of an illness was in the treatment of addiction.

Treatment at any kind of facility addresses the body, mind, and spirit by calling upon the expertise of physicians, psychologists, nurses, nutritionists, and spiritual counselors. The philosophy of a particular program is important, not whether it's nonprofit, for-profit, free-standing, or in a hospital.

The chemically dependent who have other physical or mental difficulties, such as heart disease or mental illness, are considered "dual diagnosis" cases. These patients are referred to a hospital-based center or those that specialize in dual diagnoses.

How do you find the right treatment center?

Industry experts recommend looking for a program with a variety of services that deal with the complexity of chemical dependency, and that includes detox, in- and outpatient programs, residential outpatient (halfway house), aftercare, relapse program, family therapy, A.A., and other 12-step recovery programs for patient and family.

Teens, older adults, and others with special needs should seek treatment centers that include programs specially geared to them.

As with any medical or psychological service, patients must look for programs with credentialed therapists and support staff, licensed by the state.

Private treatment centers charge anywhere from $12,000 to $30,000 (depending upon whether they're nonprofit or for-profit) for a 28-day inpatient stay. Outpatient costs range from $1,500 to

$4,000, depending upon services needed. Some nonprofit centers offer grants and loans to defray costs, and some health insurance policies cover a portion of the cost, although coverage is declining.

Employers large and small often include employee assistance programs among their benefits as supplements to regular health insurance, and have long-standing relationships with reputable treatment centers. The philosophy of these employers is that productive employees are worth the investment. Among corporate and treatment professionals alike, the attitude is that addiction is a treatable illness, and while a person has no control over their addiction, they *do* have control over their recovery.

In the section in this book on alcohol, prescription, and illegal drugs, natural detoxification methods are described, and certainly they should be part of any treatment center's physical detoxification program. Whether their use is suggested by the patient, a family member, a friend, or a treatment professional, these natural treatments should be added to the patient's program. Although they will be beneficial to the patient's detoxification and healing systems, they are *not* cures for addiction. They will detox, strengthen, and help repair damage to the body, but they will not curb the desire for alcohol or drugs. For that, we turn not only to the variety of treatment components already in use, but also to those in the experimental stages, like the promising drug ibogaine, which originated in herbal/botanical medicine.

Ibogaine is the closest thing ever to a bona fide cure for drug and alcohol addiction, yet paradoxically its curative power seems to derive from its consciousness-altering properties. Despite the government's historic queasiness about sanctioning studies of mind-active drugs, ibogaine penetrated the bias and survived to become only the second psychoactive drug to get the green light on the long road to FDA approval. Dr. Deborah Mash, a University of Miami neuroscientist who heads the team conducting the FDA human safety trials on ibogaine, says that the FDA has been very responsive regarding the drug. Dr. Mash is the latest link in the ibogaine story, but one who will bridge the gap between anecdotal evidence and scientific proof needed for FDA approval.

Ibogaine is derived from the roots of *Tabernathe iboga,* a shrub native to equatorial Africa, where tribes have long used it in small doses to remain alert while hunting and in larger amounts during sacred rituals. In 1962, heroin addict Howard Lotsof was looking for a drug high, when he tried ibogaine, but afterward, much to his surprise, found that he'd lost his desire for heroin and suffered no withdrawal symptoms. Lotsof gave the substance to other addicts, and they, too, were able to quit drugs that previously ruled their lives. As a result, The International Coalition for Addict Self-Help ran underground trial testing on ibogaine, and it was found to cure addiction to heroin, cocaine, alcohol, and other substances.

Then, underground trials began in the Netherlands in 1990, with more than three dozen addicts as test cases.

Dr. Deborah Mash was among the American scientists invited to Leiden in the Netherlands to witness ibogaine in action. She refers to it as "a chemical bar mitzvah" because of its unique actions. It's a psychoactive drug, but not a hallucinogen like LSD. It puts you into a thirty-six-hour waking dream state. During this altered state of consciousness, you relive your childhood experiences and get to the root of your addictions. In fact, ibogaine is used as a rite of passage in Africa to help tribal members make the transition to adulthood with a clean emotional slate.

Now, ibogaine is being used in essentially the same way, in effect reprogramming the addict's life. Scientists believe that by reexamining and coming to grips with childhood memories, understanding them fully for the first time, not only addiction but other emotional problems or neuroses may be solved. Dr. Mash's team stresses the belief that addiction is an illness of the spirit, and that to cure it you have to do so at the spiritual level.

Dr. Mash describes an American addict, Mark, in Holland for ibogaine treatment: "His brain was working overtime. He was viewing his past as a detached participant, observing where he went wrong, reintegrating it. He didn't want to speak or be interrupted."

On ibogaine, one may confront experiences long ago swept under the emotional carpet. Scientists have been startled to see that ibogaine cures the anxiety of decoupling from a long-term habit, prevents withdrawal symptoms, and relieves—although not completely eliminates—cravings.

"Mark went thirty days without craving, but then it started," Dr. Mash recalls. "We don't understand craving, although it's tied to relapse. An addict will tell you it's triggered by certain cues. We think it's similar to classical conditioning."

Dr. Mash is testing ibogaine's pharmacologically active metabolites, the chemicals the body makes as it metabolizes the drug. She believes that if craving returns to some extent in some people, it may be because ibogaine's metabolites have completely left the body. If so, those people may need a follow-up dose of ibogaine within a supervised treatment setting.

The only side effects to ibogaine that have been reported are nausea and imbalance at the treatment's outset, and those can be prevented and treated. In studies of monkeys given the drug Dr. Mash found no brain toxicity. "Toxicity only showed up in a study at Johns Hopkins University, and it was only toxic in near-lethal high doses that you would never give a patient," she reports.

During treatments, the team includes a neurologist, a psychiatrist specializing in addiction, and a social worker expert in "inner child" work.

The ibogaine trials are progressing so well that the drug is expected to be marketed for consumer use by the end of the decade.

Emotional and Spiritual Stress

*N*o matter the cause or situation, stress has a profound effect on your emotional, physical, and spiritual health. Stress interferes with your immune system and therefore affects your ability to fight illness and disease, from something as relatively harmless as the common cold to a host of life-threatening diseases, such as cancer. Stress is a powerful toxin.

7. Work and Money

*G*oing back to the days of the caveman, we've had to deal with stress on the job. Of course, back then, the job was to hunt down dinner before it hunted down you (and you thought *you* had it tough at work!) or taking care of cave, hearth, and family (we're talking *extremely* natural childbirth, inventing fire before you could spend all day cooking dinner, making all your clothes from the hides of neighborhood beasts, and trying to keep the kids from being eaten by said beasts).

When we humans are stressed, we instantly react physically with the "fight or flight" response, which, of course, also involves the emotions. The chemicals released (such as adrenaline) in this response cause the heart to race, blood pressure to rise, and blood sugar to soar. We are bathed in these chemicals all day, day after day, with no actual way to fight or flee. Slugging a colleague is frowned upon. So is running out the door in a frenzy. Day after day, work stresses build, and you must provide an outlet for the toxic, negative emotional buildup.

Money worries often go hand in hand with work worries, since work is how we get our money. We worry when we don't have enough; we worry when we have plenty and have to decide how to invest, protect, or spend it.

Prevention

Simplify, simplify, simplify. By whatever methods are comfortable for you, work through your old baggage, patterns, and stresses. Clean the slate. Then, approach the potentially stressful situation with the attitude that "This, too, shall pass." Defuse the stress *before* it becomes acute through direct communication, diplomacy, and the removal of fear. Remove *yourself* from all situations that are toxic to you. This will involve change, and we humans are notorious for our resistance to change, but it is absolutely necessary to preserve your physical, emotional, and spiritual health.

Antidotes

The antidotes are not only treatments but also preventive measures. You know that fight or flight routine your body and your psyche go through? Each day, you need a physical outlet for it. Daily exercise of any kind, from a leisurely walk to a full-fledged workout, gives your body a way to use those fight or flight chemicals. Think of it as your daily stress detox. Any kind of physical activity pushes your psychological reset button, clearing the day out of your system emotionally and chemically. Talking about your stress to someone sympathetic is also a healthy release.

Using any or all of the All-Purpose Antidotes presented at the beginning of Part Three will work wonders for relieving stress, particularly all forms of bodywork and massage, followed by any experiences that are soothing and relaxing to you, including meditation, listening to soothing music, aromatherapy, time outdoors, a relaxing meal with friends or loved ones—you name it. The whole point is to blast the stress out physically and follow that with a soothing, relaxing experience.

One of the wonderful things about meditation, visualization, and breathing techniques is that you can use them no matter where you are, even while at your workplace. For example, you may choose to meditate by sitting quietly at your desk, focusing your eyes on a nearby object and then clearing your mind. This will feel much like daydreaming, and it should, because daydreaming is a form of meditation. Try this method for five minutes at a time, as often as needed. Pay attention to your breathing when you use this or any other form of meditation: don't breathe faster or necessarily deeper than you normally would, just *notice* your breathing. That small act helps to calm you and trigger the body's innate healing energies. Breath is life, and when we focus on our breath we can trigger the powerful healing chemicals of our body's life force, precisely because the focus helps reduce stress and the interference stress has on our body's health.

Any other kind of "conscious breathing" technique (listening to your breath, focusing on breathing while meditating) will also clear your mind and enable you to be better in touch with your intuition, your "gut" feelings, helping you deal with stressful situations you may encounter.

Meditate and practice conscious breathing for periods of time longer than five minutes when you are not in the workplace. Fifteen minutes, twice a day, is ideal.

You may choose to meditate with a mantra (a word or phrase you say out loud or to yourself as a place to put your focus), with music, in silence, indoors, or outdoors. When you meditate, you are simply allowing your mind (and body) to calm down. Your brain waves literally slow down to what's known as the alpha state when you do any form of meditation and trigger healing mechanisms in your body, as many studies of this state have shown. Even the simple act of staring at the water, at a fire in the fireplace, or out the window is a powerful form of meditation. You know you're doing it right when it feels like daydreaming. Stray thoughts may run through your mind while you meditate, but that's okay. You might want to practice clearing your mind during meditation. You'll find that profound things can pop into a cleared mind, such as the answer to a problem you've been mulling over, or some creative or personal insight.

While meditating you may choose to picture scenes or ideas. That's what's known as visualization.

Recently, I was spending the afternoon with my brother and his family, and lounging by their swimming pool. My brother was in the lawn chair next to mine, and each of us were lying down with our eyes closed, basking in the sun.

"Open your eyes," he said, "and look straight out, but instead of seeing those trees, pretend you see the beach, and beyond that the ocean."

I followed his suggestion.

"Now, picture that all you can hear is the sound of the surf, and you're lying on this beach with someone you love, and it's just the two of you. The air is very warm, but not hot, and you are both *so* relaxed. Now, you're sipping coconut milk, and you can smell the salt air, and see a few swaying palms on the beach, and everything feels just *perfect*. The sky is robin's egg blue, with just a few wispy clouds, and the sun is strong, but not scorching, and you've never felt this good in your life!"

I didn't want that vision to end. I started adding to it, and did this for nearly a half hour. It was a powerful visualization, and I felt relaxed and lighter for the rest of the day. My feel-good feelings actually helped to trigger *more* feel-good chemicals in my brain, such as endorphins.

You can visualize with your eyes open or closed. You can do it alone and quietly, or alone, speaking out loud. You can do it with a friend or in a group.

The soothing effects of certain essential oils are ideal antidotes for ongoing, intense stress. These oils include: geranium, marjoram, lavender, basil, neroli, sandalwood, grapefruit, bergamot, and rose. Put a few drops in a bath; add oil to the melting wax near the wick of a burning candle; use in a diffuser to scent the room; add to massage oil; or dab on a tissue or handkerchief and take deep, calming whiffs (even while you're at work).

Herbal teas with calming properties, such as chamomile, can also be part of your daily stress antidote. Chamomile is perfect at the end of a busy day, and can also help you cope with stress during the day. Have a cup with lunch. It won't make you sleepy, but it will have a calming effect that will balance the stresses of the work-place.

You know that monthly Saturday afternoon or weekday evening when you sit at your dining room table or desk in the den and write all those checks for your bills? Yeah, I know . . . *ugh.* Instead of trying to counteract the stress that this ritual may produce, why not reduce the anticipated stress beforehand by using one of the following Antidotes as a preventive measure? Paying bills feels a lot better if you've just had a massage. Try balancing your checkbook or doing your taxes after a workout, brisk walk, set of tennis, game of softball, refreshing swim, or whatever physical activity you enjoy. Then sit down with your bills, checks, and pen to part with all that cash while you sip a cup of herbal tea in a delightfully scented room. No guys, this is *not* a wimpy thing to do . . . remember you just got home from one of those macho, testosterone-driving mortal combat games of tennis, or whatever it was you did with a ball of some kind. You know how relaxed you feel on a beach vacation when everything smells like coconut tanning oil? Well then, fill the room with the scent of coconut if that makes you feel good. And it's not the least bit gender-specific. Most of the essential oils are neutral in that sense, anyway. With few exceptions, they *don't* smell like grandma's perfume.

For stress-induced digestive problems, watermelon, which is al-kaline, will counteract all that stomach acid quickly and without the chemicals and possible side effects of the long-term use of over-the-counter antacids. Watermelon even works well enough to soothe ulcers.

Remember, to prevent or treat the ongoing stress that is associated with work and financial concerns, pamper yourself as much as possible. That means plenty of fresh air, sunshine, pure water, healthy food, relaxation, and fun time with loved ones. I know you don't think you have the time. Make it. Either find it or you'll be miserable for many years to come. Even a workaholic can find a way to give himself or herself permission to lead a more balanced life. Eventually you're going to do it anyway, when you're miserable enough or sick enough and realize that you really have no choice but to make changes. Don't wait until you've got migraines, the ulcer, the high blood pressure, the lousy unfulfilled feeling, or the major coronary. Do it now, and save yourself a lot of grief. An old cliché says it best: *Where there's a will, there's a way.*

> *If you were arrested for being kind to yourself, would there be enough evidence to convict you?*
> —Peter McWilliams

8. Anxiety, Worry, and Fear

Whether momentary, short-term, or long-term, these emotional and spiritual stresses can be felt immediately, emotionally, and physically. In response to anxiety, worry, and fear, our bodies release a number of chemicals, such as adrenaline and extra stomach acid, and suppress the normal efficiency of our systems, particularly the immune system.

Let's take for granted that you're already working on ways to relieve the situations that are causing you this kind of stress. Now, how can you prevent and treat the toxic effects of all this worrying?

Prevention

If you haven't read the preceding section on work and money stress, do so now. Those situations, preventive measures, and antidotes will overlap with the stresses discussed here.

It's only natural that we do a lot of worrying. Ironically, we think we're doing ourselves a big favor by worrying, that the very act of worrying will somehow help us to prevent or deal with whatever is troubling us. A little worry isn't bad—a couple of seconds of it, that is. Just enough to alert you to the fact that you have a situation to deal with. Then, instead of *worrying* about it, concentrate on a solution. Compassionate, solution-oriented thinking will actually get you somewhere. Just plain worrying will only get you upset. Don't mistake concern for worry. It's great to be concerned; for example, when a loved one is having difficulties, or when you are having any kind of problem with anything. Your attitude, however, needs to be one of healthy concern that translates into some kind of action, not unhealthy worry that translates into anxiety and stewing.

We all feel better when we're doing something about a problem, no matter how small the action may be. Action is the healthiest and most effective way to deal with anxiety, worry, and fear. In accomplishing that action, you will not only benefit by feeling good about the results of your actions, but by feeling good about making the effort to do something about what's troubling you.

From a spiritual perspective, hang on to your faith that, as the saying goes, "the universe is unfolding as it should." While it may not seem so sometimes, everything happens for a reason, and if we trust our own inner guidance, our intuition, our gut feelings, and stay open to new opportunities and experiences, we find that even the troubling situations in our lives ultimately lead to better, happier, more fulfilling and peaceful situations. Look back at some of them in your own life and see where they ultimately led. Whatever is happening now will also end up paving the way or readying us for something more positive.

The time when it's the hardest to have faith is, of course, when we need it the most. That's the whole idea of faith: it's what we hang on to when there's virtually nothing else left to hang on to. We may often feel like we're flying high in the circus tent without a net, but there *is* a net there—you just can't see it. If you dig deep down, however, you can *feel* it. That's your faith. You've felt it before when you've needed it the most. Think about it and you'll remember plenty of times. Don't let anyone discourage you, rain on your parade, or make you more anxiety-ridden. Hang on to what you sense inside, and draw strength from that.

Antidotes

The antidotes in section 7, Work and Money, will help you with anxiety, worry, and fear. Add to those the emotional and physical energy-balancing and clearing effects of bodywork, massage, and all of the vibrational medicine practices, including acupuncture, acupressure, light therapy, music/sound therapy, hands-on healing energy, and the Bach Flower Remedies. These flower essences, which exert a subtle yet powerfully healing effect, work their physical and emotional magic based upon your present emotional state.

The following Bach flower essences are antidotes for anxiety, worry, and fear:

> *Fear:* Rock rose, mumulus, cherry plum, aspen, red chestnut
>
> *Uncertainty:* Cerato, scleranthus, gentian, gorse, hornbeam, wild oat
>
> *Depondency or Despair:* Larch, pine, elm, sweet chestnut, star-of-Bethlehem, willow, oak, crab apple
>
> *Loneliness:* Water violet, impatiens, heather

Rescue Remedy, a blend of star-of-Bethlehem, rock rose, impatiens, cherry plum, and clematis, is perhaps the most recommended of the Bach Flower Remedies (all of the flower essences are available individually, and Rescue Remedy is bottled as a blend). Used as an all-purpose crisis remedy, Rescue Remedy helps to alleviate shock, mental anguish, panic, and anxiety, enabling the body's healing processes to begin immediately. It is therefore used not only for emotional crises, but physical ones as well.

Studying the universal spiritual wisdom of our native cultures provides invaluable stress antidotes. See Resources at the end of this book for a list of publications that will start you on the road or help you continue your journey of spirit.

In *Buffalo Woman Comes Singing,* psychologist and Native American spiritual teacher Brooke Medicine Eagle writes that "we must be willing to *see,* to be willing to look both at the obvious aspects of our lives, and deeper, below the surfaces of life—and to do so without denial or acting like victims. Based in our understanding that we call all our lessons to us in order to learn, we work to become aware of the influences of our past and to clear them, as well as to face new experiences with openness, responsibility and curiosity."

The idea of life as a series of lessons is central to all spiritual traditions and it is an extremely effective way of counteracting daily stresses. "One of our primary questions when faced with either an opportunity or a challenge is, 'What is the lesson here? How can I make the best use of this to learn for myself and to serve All My Relations'?" Brooke Medicine Eagle reminds us that the phrase "All My Relations" refers not only to your biological family but to all living things, and teaches us that we are indeed interconnected with absolutely everything and with the earth itself as well as the rest of the cosmos.

9. Blues, Depression, Grief, and Sudden Loss

The emotions of sadness hardly need explanation, other than to point out some of the emotional and physical differences among them. When we have what we call the blues, we experience a mood that is generally a temporary (even though it may return during another similar situation), emotional state which lasts from moments to a couple of weeks. Although the blues are marked by sadness, it is not debilitating; we can still function even though we may only be—to borrow a car analogy—running on three cylinders instead of four.

Depression is more profound; it can be temporary, lasting days or a few weeks, or long-term, lasting months or years. Reactive depression is less serious, born of our reaction to a saddening or upsetting event; it is not an inherent chemical imbalance in the brain. While many patients and physicians looking for a quick fix may be tempted to treat reactive depression with prescription drugs like Prozac, which act on the brain and come with an unfortunate array of side effects, reactive depression can be resolved with natural, gentler treatments and plenty of time for the person to process the emotions behind it. This milder form of depression is typically found in someone who has just lost a loved one, through death or the end of a relationship, or in someone who has just lost a job, suffered a financial loss, or a traumatic event.

Major depression, however, is far more serious. It can be triggered by reactive depression or emotional trauma; or it may be the result of a chemical imbalance in the brain; or it can be both. Major depression can go on for months or years and often goes misdiagnosed or undiagnosed. It can leave one barely able to get through or deal with day-to-day life, resulting in insomnia or excessive sleeping, extreme lethargy, loss of appetite, and loss of the desire to participate in life's daily activities, including work, family, and social life. Major depression is usually treated both pharmaceutically, to correct brain chemical imbalances, and with counseling therapy.

Prevention

As with the previously discussed forms of emotional and spiritual stress, the blues, grief, depression, and sudden loss take a toxic toll on the body, mind, and spirit. All prevention and antidote recommendations from sections 7 and 8, on Work and Money; and Anxiety, Worry, and Fear, should be followed. If you haven't done so yet, read those sections before continuing with this one.

Antidotes

In addition to the stress antidotes discussed in the sections, working through the blues, depression, grief, and sudden loss is most effective when done with the help of a holistically inclined psychiatrist, psychologist, counselor, or therapist.

An interesting note regarding recent research: You've probably heard of PEA—phenylethlamine—and maybe even wondered if someday science would find a way to take better advantage of what is known as our brain's love chemical. PEA, a natural amphetamine the brain makes when you're in love, turns out to be serious stuff: too little of it and your heart could quit or you could find yourself with a case of reactive depression.

A PEA compound, which has been undergoing testing in FDA therapeutic trials since 1994, could very well be the nontoxic answer for millions of people affected by a variety of depressive symptoms and states, some heart patients, and even those who are reeling from the loss of love.

Dr. Hector C. Sabelli, director of the Psychobiology Research Laboratory at Rush University in Chicago and the nation's leading PEA expert, conducted the FDA trials. He says that "if we can keep an even, healthy level of PEA in our systems, we'll be emotionally okay. People get very depressed after the loss of love, in part because of the loss of PEA output."

Previous Sabelli studies show that 60 percent of people with major depression and 100 percent of people with reactive depression have low levels of PEA. Sixty percent of those treated with a PEA compound were relieved of their depression very quickly. In the Spring 1994 issue of *Journal of Neuropsychiatry,* Dr. Sabelli reported that of the eight people given a PEA compound in a clinical study, six got well within two weeks. The effect was immediate: the depression lifted. "Most antidepressants take two to three weeks just to *begin* acting," Dr. Sabelli points out.

How does PEA work? It begins with food. We eat proteins that contain the amino acid phenylalanine. Our bodies turn the amino acid into the neurohormone phenylethlamine (PEA) in a particularly big way when something makes us feel terrific, most notably love (or at the very least lust and infatuation), and it is spread through the body. Given this brain chemical's powerful effect on our emotional well-being, you won't be surprised to learn that there is twenty times more PEA nestled in the brain than in the blood.

You can also find PEA in the heart, where it is essential to stimulate the force of contractions. After a loss of love and a severe drop in PEA, could we literally die of a broken heart. Is that what's happening when one spouse dies suddenly just days after the other? "I've seen it many times," says Dr. Sabelli, who plans a PEA heart study, "but I don't know if there's a way to scientifically relate this to PEA levels in the heart yet."

The body breaks down PEA very quickly, and its main metabolite, phenylacetic acid, is what Sabelli measures in his studies. The PEA compound that Sabelli has had so much success with, and has been studying in the FDA therapeutic trials, is a combination of PEA and the drug Eldepryl. Ingesting just PEA won't work because PEA is destroyed in the intestines and so we don't absorb much, if any, of it. Chocolate, which is high in PEA, has always been a favorite of the lovestruck and the lovelorn alike, but pigging out on it will not get enough PEA into your system to take the edge off a PEA deficiency. Eldepryl inhibits the mechanism (an MAO enzyme) that destroys PEA in the intestines and in the rest of the body. But since Eldepryl doesn't inhibit all MAO enzymes, just the offender type B, the drug is nontoxic.

PEA is believed at present to be nonaddictive. "A major component of addiction is tolerance," Sabelli points out, "and in animals as you give PEA they actually need less and less, not more and more."

Indeed, the body tends to make less PEA after we've been exposed repeatedly to the one we love over two to three years. "If you take a holiday from each other, you'll get a PEA high again," says Dr. Anthony Walsh, a Boise State University psychobiologist and author of *The Science of Love: Understanding Love and Its Effects on Mind and Body.* "This speaks well for long-distance relationships or only seeing each other a few times a week. Our experiences turn on this chemical, and when the high goes away some people say, 'The high's not there, so maybe I'm not in love anymore.' That's stupid. It's natural to stop feeling the euphoria. But we can get it back or keep it from fading by taking little breaks from each other."

Reactive depression, which can be quite strong, but is usually not long-term, is born of our reaction to a saddening event, like the loss of love or a loved one. PEA replacement therapy, which is especially effective in treating this kind of depression, may be just around the corner, allowing us to make the most of what nature has already given us.

In the meantime, chocolate comes in pretty handy for the blues or reactive depression, since chocolate triggers the release of two mood elevating brain chemicals, serotonin and endorphins and at least some PEA that manages to survive the digestion process. Digestion of chocolate and other high sugar and high fat foods that trigger serotonin and endorphins doesn't interfere with their release.

Exercise also triggers endorphins. The phrase "runner's high" describes the euphoric feeling that endorphins create. Increasing your intake of vitamin C can also help, as it is essential to the manufacturing of mood-elevating brain chemicals.

The bee products (bee pollen, bee propolis, and royal jelly) are safe, natural antidepressives. They also happen to be extremely healing since they're antibacterial, antifungal, and full of nutrients, and are used to treat and heal almost every condition and ailment you can name. You can take each separately or, for maximum balanced benefit, take them all in a combination pill that you can buy in health food stores. Bee products have been renowned for their healing, energy-boosting, rejuvenating, beautifying, and life-extending properties since pre-biblical times. Ideal as natural mood enhancers, they do not act as jittery stimulants; they are subtle yet effective. Take one pill of the bee pollen/bee propolis/royal jelly combination in the morning and, if needed, another with dinner.

10. Top Stressors: Death, Changing Jobs, Moving, Marriage, and Divorce

*K*nowing in advance that "top stressor" situations can trigger toxic emotions that will in turn affect you physically, follow the guidelines in all the sections on stress in this chapter and use them as preventive measures.

Prevention and Antidotes

With top stressors, adequate rest, proper nutrition, boosting the immune system with echinacea (described in the All-Purpose Antidotes and in section 31, *In the Spotlight:* Cold and Flu), the support of loved ones, professional counseling with a holistic practitioner, and the avoidance of toxic substances such as alcohol and drugs are more important than ever.

11. Caretaking

*T*aking care of another because you are a health care professional or a loved one can often result in serious toxic stress effects. Follow all the guidelines in each of the sections on stress in this chapter, because over the course of your caretaking you will probably feel every kind of stress.

Support groups for caretakers can now be found in nearly every community. Ask a local health professional for a reference to a group in your area. It is not uncommon for a caretaker to become almost as ill as the person being cared for because of the toxic effects of continuous stress. It is therefore most important to take special note of your own emotional, physical, and spiritual health while you are concentrating on another's well-being.

Prevention

In addition to the methods discussed in the previous sections on stress, pay special attention to strengthening your immune system with echinacea, avoid toxic substances such as alcohol and drugs, and get proper nutrition, rest, exercise, plenty of pure water, fresh air, sunshine, and quiet time alone.

Antidotes

The preventive measures are also antidotes and, in addition to the All-Purpose Antidotes and the antidotes mentioned in the previous sections on stress, pay particular attention to the use of dandelion root in tea or capsules. Dandelion root gently but effectively detoxes all of your systems, particularly your liver.

In the Spotlight

12. Toxic People and Toxic Choices

The psychological experts tell us that some people in our lives are actually toxic to us. The experts also tell us that the results of many of our choices are toxic, too.

While it may be hard to accept these statements, our bodies usually give us powerful clues long before we are willing to accept the actual cause of many emotional and physical difficulties.

"The truth shall set you free, but first it shall piss you off," Anonymous, a wise person, once said. Once we get at the truth behind our relationships and choices, and how they have affected our emotional, spiritual, and physical health for all our lives, we can begin to heal.

Healing is often spontaneous, once we've figured out the cause of the problem and removed ourself from the situation or begin actively to work on preventing the effects of the situation from manifesting in us emotionally and physically if we can't immediately leave the situation. Everyone can call upon an example of this from their own lives or the lives of someone they know: headaches that no longer plague after leaving an emotionally abusive workplace or significant other; claustrophobia that disappears once they've changed a restrictive situation; ulcers that go away when the stressful situation is remedied.

Any kind of stress interferes with your body's natural processes and natural healing mechanisms, leading to disorder, illness, and even serious disease.

How can you identify these toxic relationships and toxic choices?

It's not always easy, because Western society doesn't encourage us. We are urged to operate on logic, rather than on our healthy, intuitive sense. This causes us to stay in a situation because it may be financially secure, convenient, or filled with things we think we need, when in fact the situation is toxic to our emotional, spiritual, and physical well-being.

If, however, you listen to your intuitive sense, your "gut," you will know which relationships and choices are already or can potentially be toxic. This inner guidance is perhaps your best tool for prevention.

As important as *what* you do is *how* you do it. Make your growth and your changes in as healthy a way as possible. Avoid negative methods that merely prolong stress and anxiety, such as trying to "get even" with someone.

When you are honest with yourself and your healthy needs, you will also be positioned to prevent many toxic situations. Shakespeare's famous line, "To thine own self be true," is often quoted because it is sound wisdom. Many ancient and native peoples' wisdom have this belief in common as well, and refer, each in its own unique way, to the concept of a "higher self," which knows the truth. Whether we call it our intuition, our higher self, or our soul, since time began spiritual wisdom has urged us to listen to it.

You can employ many techniques that will help you quiet all the chatter in your head and find the truth about who you really are and which situations are healthy for you. Meditation, breathing techniques, and visualization are ideal. Yoga, which can take the form of meditation or a combination of meditation and body postures, not only works to help you clear your mind and open to healing thoughts and information, it also provides a physical release for stress in the healing benefits of stretching and movement. Denise Lardner Carmody and John Tully Carmody point out in their book, *Mysticism,* that the goal of practicing yoga "is concentration: collecting and focusing the mind and spirit. People begin the yogic enterprise scattered, distracted, the slaves rather than the masters of their minds. The first truly ambitious aim . . . is to gain control of the imagination, the feelings, and the practical reason itself."

Often some time away from a situation will help us to gain the perspective needed to understand it. Whether it's an hour-long walk or a weekend away, time removed from any toxic or potentially toxic situation is extremely beneficial as both prevention and treatment.

In *The Power of the Mind to Heal,* mind-body medicine pioneer Joan Borysenko sums up the power of your intuition, your inner voice: "Appropriate health care relies on your ability to communicate with your own wisdom, as well as with the team of professionals you hire to help you."

Natural health care practitioners can guide you through the emotional processes inherent in weeding out your life and help you treat the physical manifestations arising from stressful, toxic choices, relationships, and situations.

Just what, scientifically speaking, is this intuition? Joan Borysenko defines it in *The Power of the Mind to Heal* this way: "All information is encoded in energy waves. At times, we may receive this information through pathways other than our typical five senses. Such reception is generally called intuition."

Our intuition varies. Sometimes you may feel highly connected to your so-called gut feelings, and at other times, you may wonder where they've gone. Intuitive ability is different in each person, depending upon whether they are open to listening to their own inner wisdom, among other factors unique to every individual. But that intuitive sense is present in every human being, and the more you are aware of it and trust it, the more it will make itself apparent.

When we are in healthy, fulfilling relationships or situations, we grow, and are encouraged to grow, by the healthy people around us. If you are making changes in your life to remove yourself from toxic people or situations, you will need the support of emotionally healthy people to encourage your growth.

While change can be unsettling, the reward of emotional, spiritual, and physical well-being that awaits will make the process well worth the transition.

All of the preventions and antidotes discussed in the previous entries about stress will help you whether you are thinking about changing, are in the process of changing, or have already changed toxic relationships and situations. Read each of those entries, since those particular situations will overlap your relationships and choices.

Any time you are in the process of change, you must pay extra attention to your health, as your body's and mind's processes will be affected by the accompanying stress. You will be surprised at how much strength you can muster to deal with change, and how your body and mind, in effect, rewards you for making changes that will lead to healing. Be sure, however, to pay particular attention to boosting your immune system during this process by taking echinacea (see chapter III, section 31), following a healthy diet, getting plenty of exercise, fresh air, and sunlight, practicing meditative or relaxation techniques, and getting adequate sleep.

Talking with supportive people will help you release pent-up anger, anxiety, and stresses; it will also help you see that you are not alone in your endeavor to detox your life. The positive, loving energy you receive from supportive people will do wonders for your well-being, triggering even more healing responses in your body.

Studies have shown that our immune system is weakened by the stress hormones—adrenaline, noradrenaline, and the corticosteroids. When stress causes the release of these hormones in great quantities (and over long periods of time), we are in great danger of illness due to a compromised immune system. The stress hormones also make your heart work harder.

By contrast, our systems are also designed to reward us for cutting out the stress and surrounding ourselves with positive, loving, supportive people and situations. When we do all of that, we feel good, and the brain responds. It sends out more feel-good chemicals, such as the endorphins, serotonin, and dopamine. Add to this the fact that feeling good doesn't damage the immune system and you've got a pretty healthy reason for changing the stressful, toxic situations in your life and increasing the number of people and situations that are supportive, loving, and empowering.

Don't be surprised if, in addition to feeling relief when you make changes, you go through a grieving period for your old situation. (Read section 9, Blues, Depression, Grief, and Sudden Loss, for preventive measures and treatments.) Even when you're glad you made a change, you will still be mourning the loss of the old, and that's normal. To what extent, depends upon your circumstances. If, for example, you leave your workplace, your joy at a new opportunity might be accompanied by sadness at not seeing the co-workers who have become friends every day. Fortunately, that kind of sadness is easy to relieve: make a point to remain in contact and socialize often.

If you leave a marriage or other long-standing intimate relationship, you will probably have a mixed bag of emotions that may take more time and effort to sort through. As happy as you may be to be leaving, there will doubtless be certain things you'll miss about your former partner. Often it's possible to maintain a friendship after this kind of change, another reason to leave in as healthy and smooth a way as possible. Your total well-being will help you build an essentially new relationship with your partner, one of platonic friendship.

On the other hand, leaving a relationship where there has been physical abuse or severe emotional abuse often requires the help of professionals, both in the health care and legal professions. In this situation, a continued friendship is not desirable and not healthy.

Expect that adjustments to all changes in your life will take some time. How much depends upon your own personal circumstances. But after you have taken the steps to heal and be happy, you will be on your way to an even better future.

☙ III ☙

Environment

13. Where You Live and Work

Your level of exposure to toxins or hazardous waste is typically low, unless you live or work near a toxic site such as a chemical plant, waste dump, or mine. Toxic effect is determined by concentration and exposure. You may have a long or short exposure to low concentrations, or a long or short exposure to high concentrations.

Your body responds to toxins in two ways: with an acute or chronic response.

An acute response results from short exposure to a high concentration of a toxin. This response manifests immediately, within minutes, hours, or days of the exposure. The response is of short duration, ranging from mild to fatal.

An acute response happens, for example, if you are briefly exposed to a high concentration of a toxic substance in the environment, at work, or at home, ranging in severity from the extreme (stepping in a bucket of industrial toxic waste) to the mild (inhaling a bit of cleanser powder while you're scrubbing the sink). An acute response to short-term exposure can have disastrous consequences; it all depends upon the toxic contact.

A chronic response results from long-term exposure to any concentration of toxin (low, moderate, or high), and manifests gradually. The response is ongoing, for a longer duration—for as long as you are exposed to the toxin. A chronic response happens when you've been exposed to a toxin over a longer period of time and your body has been responding throughout the duration. Perhaps you've been exposed over time to lead in drinking water, mold in a ventilation system, chemicals in the environment, at work, in a public building, or at home. Your body will continue to respond as the toxins build with the ongoing exposure. Low concentrations of toxins can ultimately be as harmful as higher concentrations, because they accumulate in the body.

Whether you live in an urban, suburban, or rural area, you come in contact with plenty of toxins every day: pesticide residue on fruits and vegetables; bug spray; household cleaners; pet flea sprays; hair sprays and grooming products; paints, glues, solvents; plastics; formaldehyde exuded from particle board or other synthetics in furniture; dust and particles; smoke; pollen and other airborne allergens; radiation and electromagnetic fields; carbon monoxide from vehicle exhaust; chemicals in drinking water; bacteria and viruses. (If this list gets any longer, you may be tempted to go live in a glass bubble—but not plastic, since it may emit toxins, too.)

Danger from toxins is further compounded by your particular environment. If it's urban or industrial, add those particular air, water, and ground pollutants and toxins from industrial plants and traffic. If it's suburban, you're still getting urban pollution effects, unless you live in an area with little if any heavy industry that pollutes the air, soil, or water. If you live in a rural area, you may have agricultural pollutants to contend with.

How's your drinking water at home? Does the paint on your walls contain lead? What's the radon level in your house? Is there any asbestos insulation still present in an older home? How about mold and mildew? What's growing in your air-conditioning, heating, ventilation, humidifying, or dehumidifying systems? I know, that glass bubble is looking more appealing by the minute. Local government agencies can provide testing information and some services—see Resources at the end of the book.

Does your office have adequate ventilation or just endlessly recycled indoor air? Does the place you work in have "sick building syndrome" as a result of molds, bacteria, heating, cooling, ventilation, insulation, or an as yet unidentified problem? Do you work with chemicals or in an industrial environment? (For more on prevention and antidotes for those who are at extreme risk in the workplace, see section 14, Industrial Facilities.)

According to the Centers for Disease Control (CDC) in Atlanta, every year in the United States nearly one million people become sick and 900 die from drinking contaminated tap water. And more than 500,000 children have elevated lead levels from lead-contaminated drinking water.

In accordance with the Clean Water Act, the federal government monitors lakes, rivers, streams, and coastal waters. The Safe Drinking Water Act provides for the monitoring of public water systems. Congress is presently considering making some water safety standards voluntary instead of mandatory—which you may want to do something to stop (see Resources for a list of environmental action groups).

Recent studies link drinking water contaminated with high natural concentrations of arsenic to a greatly increased risk of bladder cancer, one of the nine most common forms of cancer in the United States. Some water supplies in the country contain toxic amounts of arsenic, and studies are ongoing, according to the National Cancer Institute in Bethesda, Maryland.

Prevention

Between the varieties of toxic chemicals and bacteria present in varying amounts in drinking water supplies around the country, you can significantly lower your risk of toxic exposure if you drink only bottled water (purified, distilled, or natural spring) or use a water filter and purifying system in your home.

To lessen your risk of toxic exposure to both natural and manmade toxins in the home, buy only nontoxic natural household, cleaning, craft, and gardening products, which you can easily find in natural foods and health stores or by mail through catalogs (see Resources). You may also want to make your own natural, nontoxic household products, and many books can guide you through that process (again, see Resources).

For example, Lysol, a popular disinfectant, contains derivatives of phenol and can give you a headache, especially if you're chemically sensitive. If you use a natural disinfectant product that contains a tea tree oil base instead, you will eliminate toxic exposure.

The same essential oils that are used for their healing properties also make good cleaners because they are antibacterial, antiviral, antifungal, and antiseptic, and therefore can disinfect. Most of the natural cleaners you'll find in health stores use essential oils. You can also make your own. Try this recipe for a basic disinfectant cleaner that can be used throughout the home and will also deodorize and smell good (no more harsh chemical odor!):

1. Blend a mixture of equal drops of cinnamon, clove, lemon, eucalyptus, lavender, lime, thyme, and tea tree essential oils. Store in a dark glass bottle.
2. Add eight drops of the combined mixture to two cups of water. Store in a dark glass bottle and use as needed for cleaning by dabbing the liquid on a paper towel.
3. Make more cleaner as needed from your bottle of combined oils.

The most valuable piece of prevention advice for home, office, or any location is to reduce your exposure to *anything* toxic. Since you won't be able to have a 100 percent toxin-free environment everywhere you go, you'll want to strengthen your body's ability to flush out and fight the effects of toxins released in the air, in your water, come in contact with your skin, or are taken internally. You may want to take extra precautions. Antioxidant vitamins will protect and strengthen your lungs; dandelion root will protect, strengthen, and detox your liver, as well as the rest of the cells in your body; echinacea, vitamin C, and garlic will protect and strengthen your immune system; eight glasses of pure water each day will help flush out your systems and toxins (see the All-Purpose Antidotes, for more details). Your kidneys excrete toxins that have been filtered from the blood, so drink more than eight glasses of water if you are routinely exposed to toxins, especially in the workplace. Water helps more toxins get out of the body and helps dilute the toxins as they leave the body.

Frequent exercise also strengthens your body, keeps your systems in balance, and has profound positive emotional effects.

Avoid diuretics because they dehydrate you. If you ingest diuretic substances such as coffee, tea, alcohol, or chocolate, drink more water to compensate for them.

In the workplace, take all posted and employer's suggested preventive precautions very seriously.

When working in the yard or gardening, use only natural, nontoxic products, no chemicals. You can find them at specialty stores and garden centers that carry organic products, or order by mail (see Resources).

Instead of chemical fertilizers, use nontoxic organic fertilizing materials such as cottonseed meal, fish and seaweed mixes, rock phosphate, processed animal manure, and combinations of these ingredients.

Forget about chemical pesticides/insecticides and weed-killers. Use natural ones that decompose quickly, with residues that are nontoxic:

BACILLUS THURINGIENSIS (BT). Available in dust or spray, harmless to humans, birds, and bees but deadly to pests, particularly caterpillars.

DIATOMACEUS EARTH. This is a powder made of diatoms, one-celled sea plants. It feels soft to the touch, but each grain is sharp enough to kill or at the very least severely injure insects.

HOT PEPPER SPRAY. Mix one cup of water and one cup of chopped hot peppers, let steep for twenty-four hours, strain, and add to one-half gallon of water. Put into a spray container, and use around plants, but not seedlings—it will be too harsh for them. Do not allow your skin or eyes to come into contact with the spray. It's not toxic, but it burns. It will kill most insect pests.

HOT WATER WEED-KILLER. Would you believe that after decades of scientific research, they've finally figured out that the most effective and safest way to kill weeds is to inject them with boiling water? To do this, poke a hole next to the weed and fashion a narrow tunnel down toward the weed's roots, deep enough to reach them, then pour in some just-boiled water. The hot water will instantly kill the roots, and therefore the weed. You may have to repeat the process if you haven't destroyed enough of the root the first time, but it's quick, easy, cheap, and nontoxic, so the occasional repeat procedure is no great inconvenience. Besides, even the toxic chemical weed-killers need repeat applications, and in many cases hardly work at all. Boiling your weed's roots, however, is a rather final act.

In your garden, use organic mulch and compost, rather than chemical-based toxic products, and try "companion planting," which will greatly reduce your pest problem. Certain plants planted near certain others detract harmful bugs while attracting good ones that eat the bad ones. Basil, for instance, repels mites, aphids, and mosquitoes. Marigolds, sunflowers, yarrow, cosmos, and carrots attract good bugs, such as ladybugs, that do not harm plants but feast upon those insect critters who do.

A thorough organic gardening guide can teach you everything you need to know to make your garden nontoxic, healthy, and productive (see Resources).

Antidotes

While physicians and scientists have long known that toxins cause illness and disease, they are only recently learning that toxins may underlie some addictions. Since chronic exposure to chemicals can make you feel physically and mentally uncomfortable, some people have turned for relief to recreational drugs and alcohol, not knowing that their problems are caused by a reaction to toxins. Doctors have seen this in teenage patients who have been exposed to household and occupational products whose chemicals have accumulated in toxic levels in their bodies.

To treat these patients, they must first be detoxed from the original chemicals. This form of detoxification is like the many antidotes suggested in this book, but it is conducted on a more intense, daily basis and under the supervision of a health care practitioner. The goal is to stimulate the body's excretion of toxins daily. This is accomplished by increasing intake of pure water, sweating in a steam box, massage and bodywork (particularly lymphatic drainage massage), and the use of nutritional supplements. Enzyme therapy is used to remove toxic residue from fatty tissues; from there it travels into the bloodstream for eventual elimination. Exercise is also used to strengthen the body's systems and to increase circulation and perspiration, which also help detoxify the body.

These detoxification methods are ideal for ridding the body of moderate to serious toxic buildup, no matter what the source. If you are exposed to chemicals on a continual basis, you'll want to use these antidotes on a regular basis.

As always, the preventive methods are also antidotes. For the kind of toxins you're likely to encounter where you live, work, and socialize, you'll want to add a few specific practices to the All-Purpose Antidotes and those antidotes already mentioned.

Since essential oils have such strong antiviral, antibacterial, antiseptic, antifungal, anti-infective properties, you can use them in your environment to fight those kinds of toxins. If possible, add oils to a diffuser in your work area or, at the very least, put the drops on a paper towel that you can carry with you and use to wipe down work surfaces. Lavender, geranium, clary sage, grapefruit, lemon, thyme, and rosemary are particularly effective for detoxing the air, surfaces, and *you* (when you add drops to your bath, body rub, massage oil, or a tissue to inhale). You can also wipe down surfaces with these oils at home.

Green algae drinks are effective detoxification treatments and can even tackle chemical toxins like pesticides and heavy metals. Stir one tablespoon of chlorella powder into a glass of warm pure spring water. Drink one glass each day. Any of the blue-green or green algae products—pills, powders, teas, or drinks—will work as antidotes.

If you are not feeling well and suspect that you are being exposed to toxins, put yourself under the care of a holistic physician who specializes in environmental medicine and incorporates natural treatments. Do not attempt to tackle chronic or acute toxicity on your own.

14. Industrial Facilities

*f*ollow the guidelines in the previous section 13, Where You Live and Work, and practice daily detoxification if you regularly work around anything toxic. Go above and beyond the safety precautions recommended at work, and at least twice a year visit a holistic physician who specializes in environmental medicine. Ask for blood tests and other diagnostic procedures that can monitor the levels of toxins in your body. Do not attempt to handle this on your own.

15. Radiation

*R*adiation damages your body's on-going process of cell division, DNA, your immune system, and causes cancer and radiation poisoning, which can be fatal. Many products and electronics (appliances, computers, TVs) emit low levels of radiation.

Prevention

Radiation has a cumulative effect. Get X rays only when absolutely necessary. Get mammograms using new equipment that delivers low-dose radiation (one rad/1,000 millirads). Don't buy a house or rent near a source of natural or manmade radiation, such as a nuclear power plant, nuclear waste disposal site, or a uranium mine, no matter how cheap it is and how much they try to sell you on the idea that "it really can't hurt you." It can. And it will.

Check your home for its radon gas level, particularly if you live in an area where radon levels are high in the soil. Radon usually enters your home through the basement, through cracks and pipes that permit the radioactive gas to seep up from the ground into the house. The areas at highest risk are the mid-Atlantic states, the Northwest, the Rocky Mountains, and the Southwest. Call your local health department or regional office of the Environmental Protection Agency (EPA) for information on your area and testing for radon.

Antidotes

If you have ongoing exposure (in any concentration) or short-term high-concentration exposure to radiation, do not attempt to treat the effects yourself. Immediately seek medical attention. To detoxify from sporadic low level doses, such as X rays, mammograms, and the daily low exposure from products and electronics, use the antidotes described in each entry of this chapter. All of these methods will help your systems flush out toxins. If you are undergoing or have undergone radiation treatments for cancer or other conditions, seek the help of holistic physicians specializing in environmental medicine and one specializing in radiology for medically supervised detoxification treatments.

In the Spotlight

16. Allergies and Sensitivities

*E*very spring and summer we are reminded that "the allergy season is upon us." Television commercials switch from winter's cold-and-flu runny noses to hay fever season's runny noses. And it's true: people with environmental allergies are more sensitive at this time of year.

The same plants and flowers that are feasts for the eyes can be hell on the nose. Common offenders include pollens and ragweed, but anybody can be allergic to anything, no matter what season it is. In fact, you may have allergies and be completely unaware of them. How could that be?

Medical literature and patient files give testimony to countless misdiagnoses. As more is learned about our immune system and the weaknesses responsible for the allergic reaction, many patients diagnosed with such illnesses as diverse as multiple sclerosis, irritable bowel syndrome, and even schizophrenia (plus dozens of other physical and mental conditions) are finally "cured" when at long last it is discovered that the source of the illness is actually an allergy whose symptoms mimic a particular disease. Once the offending substance is kept out of the patient's life, the symptoms retreat, and health is restored.

Plants, chemicals, and foods can cause immediate or delayed allergic reactions. The allergic process may target any area of the body and cause an array of symptoms. Holistic physicians specializing in allergy treatment see the ideal approach to treatment as a combination of detoxification, lifestyle changes, stress-reducing emotional therapy, and nutrients that can correct an immune system gone haywire.

An allergic reaction is a matter of incorrect communication within the immune system. The immune system mistakenly identifies something harmless as a threatening invader and marshals its forces, as if it were fighting a bacteria, virus, or harmful foreign body. When it kicks into high gear, it causes a range of physical, emotional, and mental responses, from itchy eyes, stuffed nose, and sneezing to hives, stomach disorder, or any number of symptoms. In extreme cases, an allergic reaction takes the form of anaphylactic shock, a potentially fatal reaction in which your blood pressure drops, tissues swell, your throat swells, and breathing difficulties follow. The treatment is an injection of epinephrine, a stimulant that in moments stops the allergic reaction and boosts the heart rate. Those who are at risk for anaphylactic shock usually carry a kit that includes a prepared epinephrine injection—to self-administer or have someone else administer. In any case, anaphylactic shock requires a trip to a hospital emergency room immediately, either for an epinephrine injection or to be checked out after it's been administered. Time is of the essence, so don't be shy about calling an ambulance if you are not within minutes of a hospital. The paramedics will administer the injection.

Although any substance can potentially cause this kind of life-threatening allergic reaction, the most common are prescription drugs, such as penicillin, bee stings, foods, and natural chemicals such as iodine, which are also found in high concentrations in shellfish and other seafood.

Once you've determined what your allergies are, with the help of holistic physicians and other health practitioners who are well-versed on the most up-to-date allergy-immunology research and methods, how can you treat them naturally?

Avoidance is the best treatment. If you are allergic to a particular food, do not eat it. Read every food label. Make sure the offending food isn't hiding as an ingredient in something else. If you're eating out and are unsure of the ingredients in a particular dish, ask, and if the answer is incomplete, don't take any chances. Skip it.

If you are allergic to substances in the environment, remove them. For instance, if you're allergic to mold, make sure your ventilation and air-conditioning system at home as well as in your workplace are mold-free. Remove mold and mildew from bathroom tiles and elsewhere in your home. Nontoxic cleaners are available in natural health stores or by mail order (see Resources at the end of this book). If you're not sensitive to chlorine bleach, you can spray or dab some onto the mold with a Q-tip. Bleach will kill mold instantly. You'll want to open a few windows while you're doing this, so the chlorine fumes can be quickly aired out.

If you're allergic to a chemical, read labels so you won't purchase products that contain something that will make you sick. And don't rely on a front label that makes promises. Read the actual ingredients list. Many food products, for example, have labels that say they're "dairy-free," but upon further inspection you'll often see a milk by-product such as casein (milk protein). If you're allergic to milk, or even have a sensitivity to it, then this isn't "dairy-free" enough for you.

In order to avoid substances that give you an allergic reaction, you must first educate yourself. Did you know that many vitamin and mineral supplements also contain lactose as a filler? If you're allergic to milk, or are lactose intolerant (missing all or some of the enzyme lactase, which digests lactose, as more than 60 percent of adults are) you'll need to know this because lactose is milk sugar.

Are you allergic to penicillin? Then stay away from Beano, a popular liquid that when added to bean dishes and other gas-producing foods reduces the gaseous effects. Beano is an enzyme called *alphagalactosidase,* perfectly harmless to most people, but since it's derived from the mold *Aspergillus niger,* it could cause an allergic reaction in people who are allergic to other mold-derived substances, like penicillin.

In some cases, complete avoidance isn't possible. Dust and pollen are going to find you unless you live in a glass bubble. While allergy shots are helpful, especially for those with moderate to severe allergic reactions, over-the-counter and prescription drugs that treat allergy symptoms do nothing to help correct the immune system dysfunction that's at the root of the allergic reaction, and these drugs frequently come with a host of annoying or even serious side effects, ranging from drowsiness to rapid heartbeat. Instead of these chemical preparations, try natural treatments (recommended in section 31 on cold and flu) for alleviating nose, sinus, and upper respiratory allergy symptoms.

Liquid cholorophyll is especially good for allergy symptoms that mimic colds and flu because it cleanses the blood and respiratory system and relieves congestion. Add a teaspoon to an eight-ounce glass of water and stir; drink once a day. When you help your body release the fluids of congestion, you are helping it to detoxify. Whether your allergy is caused by the environment (pollutants, toxins, chemicals, plants, molds, and other organisms), animals (fur, dander, feathers), or food, work with a holistic allergist who will help you to balance your immune system, minimize your contact with allergens, detox and relieve allergy symptoms.

Strengthening your systems is your first line of defense against allergies. Holistic allergists, who incorporate natural medicine into healing, recommend immune system-building nutrients, including beta carotene, vitamins C, E, and B-complex, zinc, bioflavonoids (especially quercetin), gamma linolenic acid (GLS), essential fatty acids (EFA), and selenium; herbs, including echinacea, astragalus, licorice root, Siberian ginseng, and garlic; and homeopathic allergy remedies.

Bodywork and massage, particularly if it incorporates lymphatic massage, will help stimulate, balance, and detox your systems, by promoting the draining of fluid buildup that often accompanies allergic reactions. Acupuncture and acupressure will accomplish the same, as well as normalize your body's energy flow.

Since stress so adversely affects your immune system, and it is an immune system dysfunction that causes allergies, you'll want to practice stress-reducing techniques: meditation, relaxation, yoga, breathwork, listening to soothing music, exercise and walking, gardening, playing with pets, drinking relaxing herbal teas, aromatherapy, and most important, detoxing your professional and personal life of as many stresses as possible.

In particular, the following essential oils used in aromatherapy have stress-relieving properties and can be used in a diffuser, in the warm wax of a burning candle, a simmering pot, in massage oil, in the bath, or on a tissue that you can keep with you: geranium, lavender, rosemary, lemon, rose, sandalwood, grapefruit, and bergamot. You can also use any scent you find relaxing, pleasant, and stress-reducing, like cinnamon or vanilla, which evoke the memory of the aromas of freshly baked bread, or coconut, which has the soothing aroma of a day at the beach.

❦ IV ❧

The Female Body, Mind, and Spirit

17. Breasts

In addition to the disorders, illnesses, diseases, and imbalances that result from toxic activity in your body, guess what? Now you have to worry about your bra.

You may laugh, but the bra problem is being taken quite seriously by scientists and the medical establishment, both mainstream and alternative.

In *Dressed to Kill: The Link Between Breast Cancer and Bras,* Syndney Ross Singer and Soma Grismaier write that "when we change our physical features with clothing, we change more than our appearance. We change the way our bodies work, resulting in health problems." Based on scientific medical studies, their book reports that chronic constriction of breast tissue by a bra takes its toll on the breasts, lymphatic system, and ultimately your whole body.

The lymphatic system is the part of the immune system that drains tissues of toxins and excess fluid and filters toxins out of the blood. Lymph glands that do this work are found throughout the body (see Part One, on the Immune System), and the lymph glands under each arm at the edge of each breast are prevented from properly doing their jobs by a bra. Studies show that anything that slows down or interferes with the flow of lymph fluid, such as a bra or other tight clothing, can cause accumulation of toxins in that area, which can lead to cancer. Breast cells may become malignant because the immune system processes in that area have been compromised.

Prevention

While we have long been told that bras give much-needed support to our breasts, particularly if they are large, some modifications on this line of thinking are apparently necessary. If you are small-breasted, you will find it easier to follow these guidelines. If you are large-breasted, you must take this advice seriously, and although I won't advise you to go braless in public, wear one as little as possible when you are home.

- Make sure you are wearing the correct bra size and style for your breasts. Have a professional fitting. Do not wear a tight bra.
- Never sleep with a bra on.
- Go braless as often as possible. It's easiest to do this in your own home. If you have large breasts and it is uncomfortable to be without a bra, wear a shapeless stretch bra that will hold you up without shaping or constricting.
- Wear a bra for less than twelve hours each day.
- Do self-massage of the lymph glands under each arm, next to your breasts, at least a few times each week. This is easy to do with soap in the shower or bath, or afterward, using your favorite hand or body lotion.
- Deep breathe and exercise to improve blood circulation and lymphatic circulation.

Antidotes

Use all the preventives as antidotes, and if you have been a die-hard bra wearer for many years, get a monthly professional lymphatic drainage massage in addition to your self-massage. Do this for a year, then continue with daily self-massage. If you cannot reduce your bra-wearing time, continue with monthly professional lymphatic drainage massage indefinitely. Remember to drink plenty of pure water each day to help your body eliminate toxins.

18. The Reproductive System

Toxic buildup and toxic exposure cause disease throughout the body, whether it's a system that has become toxic or a reaction to a toxin introduced from outside the body. What's the latest toxic threat to the reproductive system? A study conducted by the Environmental Protection Agency (EPA) suggests a link between endometriosis— a disease that has grown wildly, to the point where it now affects approximately 5.5 million women in the United States and Canada— and the chemical pollutant dioxin.

In endometriosis, uterinelike tissue grows outside the uterus, spreading through the pelvic area and reproductive organs as well as the abdominal cavity. The result is on-going pain and eventual infertility.

The higher the level of dioxin exposure, according to the EPA research, the more severe the endometriosis. Researchers at the University of California at Berkeley are studying endometriosis rates in women who live near a chemical plant in Italy where a major dioxin accident occurred.

Dioxin can be hard to avoid since it's a toxic by-product of many industrial processes, particularly pulp and paper bleaching and the use of pesticides. While you can do your best to reduce your pesticide intake by eating only organic, pesticide-free produce, dioxin has found its way into food, water, air, and products, particularly paper products such as toilet paper and tampons. Many paper products are now available unbleached, which greatly reduces dioxin exposure. For preventive and antidote measures regarding industrial toxins, see chapter III, Environment.

Dioxin and other toxins can also damage the reproductive system by interfering with the functions of your hormones. Hormones can themselves be toxic when they are introduced into your body in pharmaceuticals, in residues present in meats from animals that have been injected with hormones and, to a lesser extent, from plant sources.

Prevention and Antidotes

To help prevent toxicity from hormones, which can lead to a host of disorders, conditions, and diseases, and to counteract the side effects of hormones you may be taking (or ingesting in your diet), as well as any hormonal imbalance that may be present in your body, follow the All-Purpose Antidotes listed at the beginning of this part. Chinese Medicine will be especially useful, since it has always worked wonders with the reproductive system. Tackling everything from hormonal imbalances; irregular, sporadic, or heavy menstrual bleeding; cysts and tumors; PMS and menopausal difficulties; fertility problems; to preventing miscarriages, it can quickly clear up even the most persistent and serious problems and imbalances through acupressure, acupuncture, hands-on energy healing, and the use of Chinese herbal preparations.

Lymphatic drainage massage is also effective in releasing built-up toxins that can result from hormonal imbalances or excesses. Remember to drink plenty of pure water each day and eat enough fiber to help your body flush out its wastes and toxins.

Many reproductive system problems have their roots in long-buried emotional issues. You'll find that when you explore such issues with a mental health professional, deal with and release them, the physical dilemmas are soon healed, often never to return again.

If you have been taking oral contraceptives (the Pill), you'll want to remember that over time, this hormonal regimen depletes your reserves of vitamin C and the B vitamins, which can lead to cervical abnormalities and possibly cancer. To detox from the effects of the Pill, take vitamin B complex supplements and the antioxidants (vitamins C, E, and beta carotene—*Daily:* vitamin C—2,000 mg. vitamin E—400 I.U.; *Every other day:* beta carotene—25,000 I.U.) for as long as you use this form of contraception.

If you need to take hormones for any other reason, ask your physician to prescribe only hormones made from vegetable sources, not animal (see section 21, Menopause, for a complete discussion of the differences between these hormones).

If you have excess estrogen in your body, which many women do, you'll want to cut back on the sources of artificial estrogen from your diet, in particular meat and poultry, which, unless labeled hormone-free, contain residues of hormones given to the animals. Keeping your weight down will also help lower your estrogen, because the higher your percentage of body fat the higher the levels of estrogen that will be circulating. Exercise regularly—it lowers blood estrogen levels. Hormonal imbalance causes toxic effects and stresses on your body, mind, and spirit, too.

Since hormonal fluctuations cause emotional stress, be sure to read the entire chapter II, Emotional and Spiritual Stress, for background, prevention, and antidotes.

It is most important to detox your liver because it processes hormones and toxins. Drinking dandelion root tea or taking dandelion root capsules (one in the morning, one at dinner) will cleanse your liver. If you are on the Pill or other hormones, or have any hormone imbalance, you'll want to do this a few times a week, if not every day.

19. Pregnancy and Childbirth

Your body is no longer your own when you are pregnant. Suddenly you are sharing it with a growing body with a brand-new life. This developing fetus is affected by everything you think and do, and it is very sensitive to not only toxins but substances that are nontoxic to those of us who live outside the womb.

Therefore, DO NOT USE ALCOHOL IN ANY FORM, OR ANY KIND OF DRUGS. DO NOT TAKE ANY MEDICATIONS, EITHER PHARMACEUTICAL OR NATURAL WHILE YOU ARE PREGNANT, UNLESS THEY HAVE THE APPROVAL OF YOUR PHYSICIAN.

ALSO, BE EXTREMELY CAREFUL WITH SUBSTANCES YOU MAY NOT THINK OF AS MEDICINAL—SUCH AS SOME FOODS, BEVERAGES, NUTRITIONAL SUPPLEMENTS, HERBS, AND BOTANICALS. CHECK WITH YOUR PHYSICIAN BEFORE USING ANY OF THESE, EITHER INTERNALLY OR EXTERNALLY. YOU MAY WANT TO CHOOSE A HOLISTIC

GYNECOLOGIST/OBSTETRICIAN SO THAT NATURAL PRAC-
TICES CAN BE INCORPORATED INTO YOUR PRE-NATAL
CARE, YOUR LABOR, AND DELIVERY. By *natural*, I'm not re-
ferring to what's commonly known as natural childbirth—labor and
delivery without painkillers—but to the variety of natural, alternative medical methods and treatments that can be safely incorporated into pregnancy and childbirth.

Prevention

Evolutionary biologist Margie Profet recently gained a lot of attention in the medical community with her theory that morning sickness is your body's way of protecting the developing fetus from
natural or manmade toxins in food that are relatively harmless to
you, but potentially dangerous to the fetus. For example, many vegetables contain natural toxins that the fetus may not be able to tolerate, even in miniscule amounts. While you won't want to cut
vegetables from your diet while you're pregnant, you may want to
eat certain vegetables only after cooking them, which kills the natural toxins, skip a few of them entirely, and eat only organic produce in order to eliminate your exposure to chemical pesticides. For
a list of the vegetables you'll need to cook in order to kill the natural toxins, and a list of ones you may want to avoid, see chapter V,
section 25, *In The Spotlight:* Natural and Chemical Toxins in Food,
Herbs, and Supplements.

Your gynecologist/obstetrician will recommend an increase in
certain foods and vitamin and nutritional supplements. You will
need more protein, calcium, vitamins C, B, D, and E, zinc, folic acid,
phosphorus, and magnesium. Your iron intake needs to double during pregnancy.

The queasy or dizzy feeling you get during pregnancy can often
be stopped before it turns into the nausea (commonly called morning sickness, which can occur at any time of day) by drinking orange
juice. That queasy feeling is often just a low blood sugar level, and
orange juice raises blood sugar in just a few minutes. Follow the juice
by eating something light. If you can keep your blood sugar levels
even by eating something every couple of hours (smaller meals spread

throughout the day, or healthy snacks between your three main meals) you can often avoid morning sickness entirely. One of the reasons nausea is so common in the morning is that you've been asleep for hours and hours, not eating, and your blood sugar is low.

Antidotes

Detoxing while you are pregnant must be supervised by your physician. It is certainly safe to keep your body in balance, however. Encourage the natural release of toxins by drinking eight glasses of pure water each day; eat fruit and vegetables (their fiber content helps move waste products through your body for regular daily elimination); and avoid contact with natural or manmade toxins. If yours is not a high-risk pregnancy, your doctor will recommend an exercise program designed for your particular needs and limitations. A light to moderate massage will improve your circulation and encourage lymphatic drainage, which are extremely important to avoid swelling, the retention of fluid and toxins. Before having a massage, check with your doctor to make sure you are not in a high-risk category for pregnancy complications.

Certain points on your body must be avoided during acupuncture or acupressure treatments, because pressure on them can cause bleeding and/or miscarriage. Before having acupuncture or acupressure be sure to get an okay from your physician and tell the acupuncture or acupressure practitioner that you are pregnant.

DO NOT USE THE ALL-PURPOSE ANTIDOTES FOUND AT THE BEGINNING OF PART THREE IF YOU ARE PREGNANT OR SUSPECT THAT YOU MAY BE PREGNANT.

Some of the individual antidotes in that list can be toxic, dangerous, or even fatal to your developing baby. The only elements of the All-Purpose Antidotes that are safe to use without consulting your doctor (and some aren't safe even with a doctor's supervision), are those I've mentioned here: plenty of pure water and adequate fiber in your diet. Everything else, even exercise and massage, must first be okayed by your doctor. For example, the immune system–boosting herb, echinacea, cannot be taken if you are pregnant, unless recommended by your health care practitioner. Many other herbs can cause damage to the fetus, uterine contractions, or other internal actions that are extremely dangerous to the fetus.

Plenty of natural or alternative medicine treatments and practices are perfectly safe to use when you are pregnant, depending upon your particular body. They can be recommended by a holistic practitioner, in conjunction with the supervision of your gynecologist/obstetrician.

Here are two alternative treatments that are perfectly safe and effective:

- For queasiness and nausea during pregnancy: Press the acupressure point known as Pericardium 6, which is located on the inside of the wrist between the two tendons two inches from the wrist crease (going in the direction of your arm). You can buy wristbands especially designed to put pressure on this point; ask at pharmacies or natural health stores. These are the same wristbands used to prevent and treat seasickness and are popular with those who take cruises.
- For constipation during pregnancy: Squeeze half a lemon into one cup of warm water and drink it in the morning. Lemon water stimulates the intestines to contract gently, which in turn, stimulates elimination.

Because your growing womb will be pressing more and more against your bladder as your pregnancy progresses, urinating will become a frequent pastime, but daily bowel movements may become less common or more difficult. It is very important that your body eliminates its waste and toxins, and that means you need to have a bowel movement at least once a day. Another gentle way to stimulate elimination is by eating prunes, raisins, and other dried fruits.

During the late stages of your pregnancy and during labor and delivery, you may want to sip burdock root tea. Check with your holistic health care practitioners and doctor first. It has long been safely used during these times, since it detoxes and balances your systems. Burdock root is high in iron, which your body needs a whopping dose of during pregnancy. If your iron levels are too high, don't use it. Sip a bit of the tea throughout the day, but don't drink more than a total of two cups per day. Just after delivery, it is very healing. Labor and delivery are major stresses to your body, and you will be dealing with their effects immediately afterward, in the postnatal time, and in the following months.

20. Postnatal

*D*uring the first year after you give birth, your body will be healing, your hormones will be readjusting, and gradually you'll return to a physical state similar to before you were pregnant. There are still stresses on your body, mind, and spirit in this postnatal time, especially if you are breast-feeding, experiencing the severe form of postnatal blues that are caused by fluctuating hormones, or if you had any pregnancy, labor, or delivery complications. Although you are no longer carrying a fetus that can be harmed by toxic substances, you should still consult with your health care practitioners when choosing natural or alternative practices or treatments if you are breast-feeding, because substances you ingest are passed to your baby through your breast milk. For that reason, you will also want to continue to be extra careful with exposure to the toxins with which we all routinely come in contact in our environment and food.

Prevention

You may resume the use of the All-Purpose Antidotes as preventive measures, but get okays from your health care practitioners before you take nutritional or herbal products if you are breast-feeding. To help clear your body of toxins and excess fluids, restore your systems to a balanced state, and help your body deal with hormone readjustment, bodywork and lymphatic drainage massage are recommended. The vibrational medical practices, particularly acupressure and acupuncture, will help your body restore a healthy energy flow and assist in processing your hormonal changes.

Chinese Medicine, with its use of hands-on energy healing, acupressure, and acupuncture, is especially effective in treating gynecological problems and restoring gynecological health and balance. It also detoxes your body from the effects of hormonal fluctuations and returns the hormones to balanced, pre-pregnancy levels.

If you are breast-feeding, your doctor will advise you regarding your nutritional vitamin and supplement needs.

Antidotes

As is often the case, the preventive measures are also antidotes. To counteract the physical and emotional stresses of this first year (not to mention motherhood!), pay particular attention to the pampering your body requires while you heal. You need plenty of rest, ironically, at a time when it's almost impossible to get any. Do whatever it takes to assure that you have restful periods and get as much sleep as possible. Sleep deprivation is common when you have a newborn who wakes up a number of times during the night. If you can, catch catnaps during the day when the baby is sleeping. The toxic stress that is placed on your body by sleep deprivation is enormous. Call upon friends and family to help as much as possible so you can rest and heal. Don't feel guilty about doing this. Allowing yourself to become ill is not going to do your baby any good, so don't play martyr.

Consult with a physician trained in Ayurvedic medicine regarding detoxing treatments and nutrition, which can be particularly helpful as your body processes all those postnatal hormones.

21. Menopause

Although the average age for entering menopause is fifty-one, plenty of women are premenopausal or begin menopause in their mid- to late forties.

During menopause your reproductive hormones (estrogen and progesterone) decline, and you will ultimately stop menstruating and lose your ability to conceive. While it seems like it should be a simple process, unfortunately, it is accompanied by a number of potentially difficult physical and emotional effects that range from mildly annoying to life-threatening. No, you can't die from menopause, but the synthetic hormones commonly prescribed to replace the natural ones that you now produce very little of, can put you at higher risk for cancer and other diseases.

Menopause can be a calm, safe, healthy, nontoxic transition. And the more you rely on natural products, the healthier you will be.

First, let's look at what happens with your hormones every month and how menopause affects that process. Estrogen is produced by your ovaries. It regulates your menstrual cycle, prepares the uterus for receiving a fertilized egg by stimulating the uterine lining to grow, and also affects all of your body's cells. Your natural estrogen level permanently declines with menopause. Progesterone, which is also produced by your ovaries, comes into play mostly after ovulation. When you are not pregnant, your progesterone level rapidly declines, causing your uterine lining to shed, which is your monthly period. With menopause, your natural progesterone level permanently declines to the point where your body only makes very little of the hormone.

Because estrogen and progesterone levels sink so low, many changes happen to you at the onset of menopause: vaginal dryness and shortening, hot flashes, mood swings, fluid retention, osteoporosis (estrogen protects you from losing calcium, so with only a little estrogen your bones may become brittle and your posture hunched), heart disease (normal levels of estrogen also lowers your risk), lined and dry skin, vaginal and urinary tract infections, excessive bleeding as you enter menopause, and insomnia.

These effects are toxic to you, but unfortunately the usual remedy prescribed by mainstream physicians can be even more harmful. There are safer ways.

Prevention

Most women entering menopause choose some form of hormone replacement therapy (HRT) to add estrogen and progesterone back into their systems and offset the toxic effects of menopause. The effects of conventional synthetic, animal-derived hormones prescribed by your doctor, however, are increasingly alarming, so more and more women are choosing natural, plant-derived hormones and other natural treatments instead.

Hormone replacement therapy does lower your risk for or prevents (depending upon your medical history) heart disease and osteoporosis, and prevents or relieves the rest of the long list of menopausal side effects. However, the synthetic, animal-derived hormones in a typical prescription raise the risk of breast cancer, and estrogen alone, without a progesterone supplement, raises your risk of uterine cancer. These mainstream prescriptions also cause weight gain, water retention, unwanted hair growth, patches of skin discoloration, higher risk of blood clots, depression, liver damage, increased risk of gallstones and gallbladder disease—the list keeps growing.

Why? Because the hormones in these mainstream prescriptions are not natural to humans. A woman's body makes three kinds of estrogen: estrone (E1), estradiol (E2), and estriol (E3). The most commonly prescribed estrogen replacement, Premarin, is made from the urine of pregnant mares (the source of the name). This horse urine contains approximately twelve estrogens, only two of which match a woman's type of estrogen. Even knowing so many of the bad effects of synthetic, animal-derived hormones, we still don't have enough test information on what the other ten horse hormones do to a woman's body. For patenting purposes, most of the synthetic hormones have also been altered, so much that they no longer match human hormones. For instance, Provera, medroxyprogesterone and Agestin, commonly prescribed as progesterone replacements, don't match human progesterone, so they will upset your hormone balance, cause side effects, and fail to do progesterone's most important job—preventing osteoporosis by stimulating bone density.

Estratest, a synthetic estrogen replacement, contains methyltestosterone, which causes liver and cardiac damage. It isn't recommended that you take another commonly prescribed estrogen replacement, Estrace, either, due to risky side effects.

Remember the three kinds of estrogen women's bodies make? In estrogen replacement you can't just use equal amounts of each, because that's *not* how they would have been naturally produced in your body. In any prescription for estrogen replacement (whether it's synthetic, animal-derived, or natural, plant-derived), estrone (E1) and estradiol (E2) should be used in lower doses than estriol (E3), because they are associated with increased cancer risk. Estriol (E3) should be at a higher level in the mix; it has the beneficial effect of being safer, healthier, and able to shrink fibroids and lower cancer risks. Estrogen from any source that is given alone, not in conjunction with progesterone, may increase the risk of uterine cancer. Progesterone must also be taken.

By using only plant-derived hormones in hormone replacement therapy, you can prevent and treat all menopausal symptoms without the risky side effects of synthetic, animal-derived hormones. Ask your physician to prescribe only plant-derived medications for you. These natural medications are made from such vegetable sources as soy, which is rich in phyto-estrogens and will act in your body like the estrogen you would normally produce; wild yam, which provides progesterone; and others.

Estrogen and progesterone are most effective when delivered into your systems through your skin by applying them in cream form. When you take hormones in pill form, 90 percent of the hormones are destroyed by your liver and only 10 percent actually get into your bloodstream. Not only does this not supply the hormone level you need, but it puts a toxic burden on your liver. Hormone creams are rubbed on your abdomen, below your navel, right over the uterus. You'll need to use a progesterone derived from a plant source other than wild yam in a cream, because wild yam can't deliver progesterone through the skin. (See Resources at the end of this book for product information). Your physician can write prescriptions for pills or cream, or order from a number of sources throughout the country, which are listed at the end of the book in Resources. You will need a prescription in order to get plant-derived hormone replacement therapy.

In addition to hormone replacement therapy, you can take additional preventive measures to deal with menopause and its immediate effects and lower your risk for future difficulties. For those who have breast cancer, uterine cancer, uterine fibroids, liver disease, or blood clotting problems and therefore may not be using hormone replacement therapy, you'll need to rely on these other natural prevention techniques and antidotes even more.

Exercise, including weight training, Nautilus, walking, running, aerobics, etc., proper diet, and calcium supplements help prevent osteoporosis—a fact you'll want to keep in mind long before menopause.

Chinese Medicine's herbal teas and mixtures, acupressure, and acupuncture work extremely well for anything concerning a woman's reproductive system, including preventing and treating menopausal effects.

Consult with a naturopathic doctor or other holistic health care practitioner who can create an herbal program for you. Using a balance of what's known as estrogen and progesterone precursor herbs (they have an estrogenic or progesterone effect on your body and promote production of these hormones) can be beneficial. Estrogen precursor herbs include: dong quai, black cohosh, alfalfa, ginseng, licorice root, anise seed, fennel, garlic, papaya, red clover, and sage. Progesterone precursor herbs include sarsaparilla, chaste berry *(vitex agnus cassus)*, wild yam, and yarrow. They will help your body produce only the hormones it needs, never more than what it needs.

DO NOT TAKE BIRTH CONTROL PILLS TO PREVENT OR TREAT MENOPAUSAL SYMPTOMS AND EFFECTS. In general, the safety of these drugs is questionable for women over the age of thirty-five, and they contain higher levels of estrogen than are needed during menopause, which means an increased risk of ovarian and breast cancer. This particular mix of hormones also suppresses the activity of your pituitary gland.

Antidotes

Preventive measures are also used as antidotes. In addition, you may want to mimic the cycle you had before menopause by taking four to seven days off from hormone replacement therapy every month, giving your body a time of low estrogen and progesterone levels, just like when you had your period. This hormone "fast" will help you detox from the hormones (whether they're the synthetic, animal-derived or the plant-derived), just as your body used to do for a few days each month before you entered menopause. Plan this kind of hormone schedule with your physician or holistic health care practitioner.

To treat vaginal dryness, use a natural internal lubricant, and remember that during lovemaking, both foreplay and intercourse naturally stimulate lubrication and blood circulation to the vagina. Exercise also increases blood circulation to the entire pelvic area, which helps to nourish tissues. Chaste berry *(vitex agnus cassus)* is also effective for revitalizing vaginal tissues. Take one capsule up to three times a day on an empty stomach, or put 20 drops of the liquid tincture in a cup of water, tea, or juice, and drink twice each day (each cup containing 20 drops).

For mood swings, vitamin B complex, vitamin E, beta carotene, magnesium, potassium, and zinc are helpful. You can find vitamin supplements especially designed for menopause that have a blend of the most beneficial vitamins, minerals, nutrients, and herbals. Ginseng helps balance moods, and the bee products (bee pollen, bee propolis, and royal jelly) are known for a wide array of health benefits, including their antidepressive effects. You can buy pills that contain all three bee products blended together. Take one each morning, and another with dinner if needed. Because the bee products also provide a gentle energy lift (without overstimulating or increasing your heart rate as a stimulant herb like ephedra does), you may not want to take them after 8:00 P.M. if you have insomnia or difficulty sleeping. Otherwise, you can take them in the evening without any difficulty.

Herbs that are beneficial for all menopausal effects include: dong quai, ginseng, raspberry leaf (which helps normalize your entire reproductive system), and dandelion root and milk thistle to help your liver detox your systems. Follow the directions on the labels of these products.

Remember to drink plenty of pure water each day to flush out toxins, which is extremely important if you are taking any kind of hormone replacement therapy. You'll also want to lower the amount of oils and fats in your diet (except olive oil), in order to take more pressure off your liver, which is quite busy processing all these hormones.

All forms of bodywork and massage, especially lymphatic drainage massage are important during menopause, as they help pump out the toxins, fluid accumulation, and hormones. Remember, you used to have a period every month that did this automatically. Now, you'll need to help your body along in this vital monthly process. You'll find that if you do this, many of your symptoms will reduce dramatically, and often disappear entirely.

In the Spotlight

22. PMS

*L*et's talk about that delightful time of the month when women get bloated, cranky, weepy, anxious, queasy, blue, and yucky. No, those are not the names of the Seven Dwarfs, and yes, you guessed it, we're talking about PMS, premenstrual syndrome, which we look forward to about as much as the prospect of being nibbled to death by ants while being audited by the IRS.

In the spirit of participatory journalism and authenticity, I was hard at work on this section while in the throes of PMS. As I write this, PMS is behind me now by about a week, and I can literally feel my hormones stabilizing and my lust for chocolate subsiding. I haven't shed a tear since Saturday.

Every woman who experiences PMS—it's estimated that one-third to one-half of us feel its effects—does so in her own unique way. It's like ordering from a Chinese menu. Your body chooses its symptoms: some from column A, some from column B, some from column C. But the good news is that you can treat, prevent, and even eliminate PMS symptoms safely and naturally by adding or eliminating foods, using herbs, exercising, and using massage and other techniques that balance, detox, and heal. In most cases, you can live in harmony with your swirling hormones without taking prescription or over-the-counter pharmaceuticals, except perhaps for a light painkiller. Tylenol, buffered aspirin, or ibuprofen work for the cramps or headaches that may come at the end of PMS and the onset of your period, when you aren't yet responding to your new natural regimen.

During the second half of your menstrual cycle—the fourteen days preceding the first day of your period—the hormones estrogen and progesterone increase, setting the stage for many of the PMS symptoms. The increase in these hormones, coupled with the imbalance between the two causes mayhem in your body and mind.

Estrogen and progesterone have opposite effects on the brain. If your estrogen is higher during this time, you'll feel anxious. If your progesterone wins out, you'll feel depressed. The balance between these two hormones depends on how much of the hormone is produced and in which way it is disposed. On their way out of your body, these hormones make a stop at your liver and then your kidney, which prepares them for the grand exit of liquid and solid elimination. Emotional stress and nutrition greatly affect this process. Excess fats and sugar keep your liver much too busy to process the hormones effectively, too. The result? The hormones continue to circulate in your body instead of leaving it in balanced amounts. You can help your liver with its processing job by drinking a cup or two a day of dandelion root tea, which detoxifies the liver and boosts its efficiency.

Meanwhile, elsewhere in your body, other processes contribute to the creation of an environment for PMS symptoms to flourish. Your body is much more sensitive to insulin during this time. This means that insulin essentially works too hard, allowing more sugar to leave the bloodstream and enter the cells than at other times of the month. When this happens, your blood sugar level drops. With less glucose sugar circulating in your blood, there is less available to the brain, and as glucose is the body's number one fuel, the brain responds with a cry for more fuel. Your body translates this cry into an increased craving for sweets. If you're under emotional or physical stress, the situation worsens, because your brain wants even more fuel, and you respond to that with a desire for even more sweet goodies.

Your brain makes a number of chemicals (neurotransmitters that transmit messages from one brain cell to another) that elevate your mood. Among these so-called feel-good chemicals are serotonin and the endorphins.

During the last two weeks of your monthly cycle your serotonin level drops, hitting its lowest a few days before your period begins. The PMS blues that begin just after ovulation, and gradually worsen, are in part caused by this serotonin drop.

The endorphins escalate at ovulation for about forty-eight hours. And, since they also increase your sex drive, this is your body's way of putting you in a great mood *and* a romantic mood when you are at your most fertile time, setting the stage for passion and the possibility of sperm and egg creating a new life. The endorphins then drop back to their normal levels. Even though they don't go below their usual level, you really enjoy that 48-hour peak, and physiologically you go into a withdrawal from it. This blues-producing withdrawal continues through the premenstrual days, right up through your period. The withdrawal from this endorphin high can also make you lethargic and anxious.

Serotonin is released in your brain after you eat carbohydrates, and the endorphins are released after you eat fat and carbohydrates. The carbohydrates and fats combined in chocolate triggers the production of both chemicals. During your period and in anticipation of it, your clever body looks for ways to get what it needs. A craving for chocolate and other feel-good foods take the edge off some PMS symptoms because these foods push the buttons to release feel-good brain chemicals.

Without proper nutrition and vitamins in your diet, your PMS problems will be magnified. Without the proper nutrients, especially magnesium and vitamin B in your diet or supplements, your body can't convert sugar into fuel. That's another reason why you reach for chocolate. It's high in magnesium. What you're doing, even without being consciously aware of the chemical makeup of chocolate, is satisfying your body's urgent needs at the moment: more sugar, more magnesium, and some phenylethylamine (PEA), which has an antidepressant effect, and the aforementioned antidepressant effects of serotonin and the endorphins. Chocolate also has a fair amount of iron, and if you're iron-deficient that will add to your craving since the loss of blood during menstruation reduces your iron level.

While we're on the subject of iron, it's a good idea to have a standard blood test yearly (see chapter X, Times of Life, section 50, *In the Spotlight:* Annual Physicals Timeline) to monitor your red blood cell count and, therefore, your iron levels. A low red blood cell count, anemia, means an iron deficiency.

In the interest of maintaining a healthy diet, I decided nearly two years ago to cut red meat out of my diet. Prior to that, I'd been eating it only a few times a week, and only lean cuts. I continued to eat chicken, turkey, and seafood, but no beef, pork, or game. Since I took a multivitamin nearly every day, ate no dairy, very little fat except healthy olive oil, and plenty of fresh vegetables, I thought I'd be just fine. . . . *Wrong.*

Now, for some people, this diet could have been fine. I just happened not to be one of those people, and I didn't know it. Gradually, my stores of iron were depleted, and after about a year of no red meat (which is very high in iron), I began feeling sluggish and tired, and looked pale, despite my freckles and plenty of sunshine. I didn't make the connection, though, to the lack of red meat in my diet. I should have been making sure that I got plenty of extra iron to replace what I would have gotten from the red meat. Even though I was eating a healthy diet, I should have been paying particular attention to the high-iron vegetables and other non-red meat sources and eating more than the usual amounts of those. In fact, during this time I heard a lot about how many Americans actually have too much iron in their systems because so many of our prepared foods (cereals, breads, and the like) have been iron-enriched. I never checked my blood levels after I quit eating red meat. All I knew was that they were in the midrange of normal about five years before, when I'd had my last complete blood test.

Lo and behold, just recently I found out that I was anemic, meaning my red blood cell count was well below the bottom of the normal range. I had a routine blood test as part of a physical, and suddenly it all made sense to me. I'd been feeling so tired and looking so pale because I had an iron deficiency.

What are your options if you are anemic? Iron supplements

often cause uncomfortable side effects: constipation, diarrhea, nausea, headaches. I decided to skip those. I'm taking a multivitamin that gives me 100 percent of the RDA for iron, but that's not enough, since I have a lot of catching up to do. So, I went back to red meat. That may not be everyone's first choice, but I decided it would work best for my system. Once my iron levels are back where they belong, which will take a few months, I'll only eat red meat a few times a month and will get extra iron from cooked spinach (about a cup has 20 percent of the recommended daily allowance), plus white meat chicken, potatoes, and other foods with a substantial amount of iron. Right now I'm eating some lean steak every day, and enough spinach to make Popeye proud. After only five days, I feel much better already. And I look better, too.

Many women report that just before, during, or just after their period they crave red meat, even though they may not each much, if any, red meat in their normal diet. If this happens to you, or if you eat little or no red meat, or you're feeling tired during PMS or at any time of the month have a blood test and make sure you aren't anemic and iron-deficient. Since we bleed every month, for years and years, we're regularly losing iron in those red blood cells that leave our bodies for two to five days at a time.

Other forces are also at work contributing to PMS. The pituitary gland is secreting more of the hormone ACTH at this time of the month. It travels to the adrenal glands, which then send out their own hormones on a trip to the kidneys. The kidney's response is to hold on to its salt and water. This means bloating, tender breasts, and weight gain of up to a couple of pounds.

The busy body, a master at doing a million things at once, is also playing host to more than the usual amounts of androgens. These elevated hormones, generated by the adrenal gland, are what's behind changes in the skin's pH balance and an increase in the skin's oil secretion. The results are blackheads, whiteheads, or pimples.

The uterus also gets into the act, producing prostaglandins. Just before and during your period, if the uterus's nine kinds of prostaglandins are not balanced, look out. When there's more prostaglandin type II than type I, you'll experience cramps, lower back pain, and queasiness or nausea. Some light cramps during your period may be unavoidable, no matter what preventions or antidotes you take, simply because your uterus contracts as it flushes out its lining.

Prevention and Antidotes

As always, prevention is a big part of the answer to any question about your body's imbalances. Let's take it one major symptom at a time.

ANXIETY, IRRITABILITY, OR SNIPPINESS. You have too much estrogen. Hormone activity is heavily influenced by what you eat. The higher the fat content of your diet, the more estrogen you'll produce. Some foods also bring estrogen into the body, like meat and poultry. Animals receive hormones to fatten them up and pass them directly to you when you eat them. A vegetarian diet has been shown to make a big difference in eliminating excess unwanted hormones, specifically estrogen. Soybeans and soy products contain a natural estrogen, as do some other nonmeat foods, so if the effects of soaring estrogen during PMS are taking their toll on you, you'll want to cut back on all dietary sources of estrogen, particularly during PMS time. Eat meats that come from animals that haven't been given hormones. You can find them at specialty stores and certain butchers.

DEPRESSIONS, THE BLUES, WEEPINESS. Your progesterone is soaring. Fortunately, it will take a nosedive as your period begins. Physicians, researchers, and holistic practitioners have finally come to the conclusion that it's healthy to indulge your carbohydrate cravings during this time because of the beneficially calming, happy neurotransmitters (brain chemicals), particularly serotonin, that are produced in extra amounts when you eat carbohydrates. Instead of bingeing all at once, though, try nibbling on small amounts throughout the day to keep the levels of the neurotransmitters constant. Go for what makes you feel the best, whether it's chocolate, bread, pasta, potatoes, or any other high-carbohydrate food. For mood swings, you'll want to eliminate alcohol and dairy products. If you can tolerate a little caffeine (a few sips of coffee or a half a glass of cola), it will elevate your spirits. So will the bee products (bee pollen, bee propolis, royal jelly) since they're safe, natural antidepressants that are also extremely healing.

CRAVINGS. What do you do if you're craving sweets? Big boosts of sugar will only make your craving worse, so eat sweeter foods than white sugar, but in small quantities. Honey and maple sugar work well.

BLOATING. If you're bloated and your breasts feel tender, eliminate as much salt as possible from your diet during the fourteen days before your period. This will prevent water retention almost entirely in many cases. If you haven't taken enough salt out of your diet, or you're bloated anyway, try Traditional Medicinals' PMS Tea. Its safe and natural herbs include those that act as gentle diuretics. Raspberry leaf tea balances a woman's system and is highly recommended not just for PMS, but all month long.

BLEMISHES. To prevent blemishes, increase your intake of food sources of vitamin A. Carrots, sweet potatoes, broccoli, apricots, peaches, asparagus, kale, and salmon are among the best to choose from. The carotene present in these vitamin A-rich foods nourish, cleanse, and balance your skin.

CRAMPING, BACK PAIN, AND NAUSEA. These ailments can be prevented and relieved by ginger tea or ginger capsules. Increasing your intake of calcium and magnesium will also help.

Moderate, regular exercise increases overall muscle tone. Strengthening the back and abdominal muscles can help prevent cramps and lower back pain associated with PMS and your period, too. Yoga stretches can work wonders for preventing and relieving pain and stress, reducing swelling and fluid retention, and stimulating regular elimination.

A good back rub, neck rub, or full or partial body massage relieves pain, stress, and contributes to your peace of mind. The therapeutic and relaxing effects of professional acupressure, lymphatic drainage, Swedish, or neuromuscular massage are almost miraculous. A professional massage costs between $20 and $80 per hour depending upon where you live, the type of treatment, and whether the service is offered by a massage school, private therapist, or a spa.

The regular practice of meditation clears the mind, calms the soul, and nourishes the body. You'll need all of that in your PMS prevention and treatment routine. The premenstrual time adds stress to the body and mind, often making life's already major annoyances even worse, so take a deep breath and relax.

Pamper yourself, be kind to yourself during this time. Try soothing aromatherapy, bubble baths, an enlightening book, a funny movie, beautiful music, a long talk with someone close, cuddling, plenty of fresh air and sunshine, a walk on the beach or down a country road, a day in the park. If it helps to have a good cry, do it. Release everything. What we bottle up eventually turns toxic in our systems.

Essential oils for aromatherapy and healing that are recommended during this time include lavender, rose, and geranium. Add a few drops of each to your bath, the melted wax of lit candles, or a room diffuser.

The ancient Chinese herb dong quai *(Angelica sinensis)* is considered the ultimate woman's herb and is excellent for all PMS symptoms. Herbalist and author Rosemary Gladstar Slick recommends the following dosage: On the first day after your period has completely stopped, take two 530 mg. capsules three times per day. Stop taking dong quai when your period begins. The herb stimulates blood flow to the pelvic area and can increase bleeding.

Improvements in how you feel during your premenstrual time can be gradual or surprisingly quick, and some months may be better than others, but by getting to know your body and mind you can control PMS naturally instead of it controlling you.

V

food

23. Overeating, Digestive Problems, Imbalanced Diet, and Eating Disorders

food is the fuel and the medicine that makes our bodies function, stay well, and heal. But food can also cause disruption, disease, and toxicity.

An imbalanced diet, overeating either periodically or regularly, and eating disorders such as bulimia (overeating followed by self-induced vomiting) and anorexia (self-starvation) can all have toxic, even disastrous effects.

Prevention

In theory, preventing overeating, digestive problems, an imbalanced diet, and eating disorders looks easy. In practice, however, it is often difficult because our relationship to food is so closely tied to our emotions. We tend to fill emotional and spiritual emptiness with food; we use food as a reward and overindulge; we deprive ourselves of food in order to either achieve what we or society tell us is the perfect, slim physique or to have some sense of control over our bodies and, by extension, our lives; we also purge our bodies of food so we won't retain it and possibly gain weight.

If you occasionally overindulge—for example, on weekends, holidays, or special occasions—you can deal with that far more easily than if you have a serious overeating problem or an eating disorder. Occasional or chronic digestive problems are usually linked to stress, underlying illness, a food allergy or sensitivity, food poisoning, overeating on a particular occasion, reaction to medication, ineffective processing and elimination of food/waste/toxins, or indigestion from rich, spicy, or difficult-to-digest foods. An imbalanced diet can be corrected by educating yourself and/or consulting a holistic nutritionist or other holistic health care practitioner qualified to provide individualized nutritional counseling.

If you are more than twenty-five pounds overweight, consult with a holistic health care practioner who can help you design a nutritionally sound eating program. Fad diets either work temporarily (it's estimated that 90 percent of those who go on such diets gain the weight back) or don't work at all. If you are not responding to the sensible, long-term diets, it's time to consult with a holistic health care practitioner.

If you are seriously obese, you are in a potentially life-threatening situation. One hundred extra pounds or more puts an enormous strain on every system in your body, and often leads to diabetes, stroke, heart disease, and heart attacks, among other disastrous effects. Putting yourself under the care of a holistic physician will enable you to restore your health under supervision, and guide you through a weight-loss program.

If you, or someone close to you, have any kind of eating disorder, seek professional medical help immediately. Do not attempt to treat it on your own. Eating disorders are severely debilitating and potentially life-threatening.

For occasional overeating or digestive disturbances and an imbalanced diet, make every effort to maintain a balanced diet without overdoing it. Ayurvedic medicine suggests that after eating, take a ten- or fifteen-minute rest, lying on your left side. The stomach hangs to the left, and when we lie on that side, food can be processed more efficiently, and indigestion and heartburn can be prevented. Because human digestion is slow compared to that of other meat-eating animals, meat often putrefies in our intestines and releases toxins in our bodies. Eat plenty of fiber and drink at least eight glasses of pure water each day so that you will have at least one bowel movement a day and will urinate several times each day.

Antidotes

In addition to the use of preventive measures as antidotes, follow the All-Purpose Antidotes listed at the beginning of Part Three that pertain to food and elimination such as adequate fiber, water, and bodywork. Ayurvedic medicine incorporates many digestive treatments, such as this one to aid digestion and eliminate toxins: Drink a tea made of a pinch of cardamom powder added to one cup of warm water after a meal or whenever you are experiencing digestive problems. Small amounts of ginger and turmeric also stimulate digestion and remove toxins. They can be added as spices to food or made into teas by adding a teaspoon of ginger or a pinch of tumeric to a cup of warm water. Ginger tea can also be found in tea bags or as loose tea.

Essential oils can help relieve constipation. Mix 15 drops of rosemary, 10 drops of lemon, and 5 drops of peppermint essential oils into two tablespoons of massage oil or cream (such as Eucerin cream or plain vegetable oil), and massage in a clockwise motion over your lower abdomen three times per day.

Simple nausea can be relieved by ginger tea or ginger capsules.

If you suspect that you have food poisoning, seek medical attention immediately.

Enemas and other invasive forms of elimination-tract and colon cleansing can be risky because of their often harsh, sudden, and drastic effects on the body. Use invasive measures only when absolutely necessary and under medical supervision. Colonics can also result in internal infections. If you need to stimulate a bowel movement, do so gently with prunes, prune juice, or other dried fruits, a bran muffin, raisin bran, or other high-fiber cereal taken in small to moderate quantities. You do not want to induce gas, cramping, or diarrhea, and all three will happen if you ingest some of the many teas or high-fiber concoctions on the market that are advertised as "cleansing" or bowel movement–inducing.

If you are having chronic elimination problems, see your holistic health care practioner. The cause may be in your diet or as a result of some underlying condition.

FASTING. If you would like to fast periodically to cleanse your system, do not do so for more than three days at a time, unless you are under the supervision of your holistic health care practitioner. Periodic short fasts—one day per month, one day four times per year—should include at least eight glasses of pure water a day, and plenty of fruit and/or vegetable juices.

Before any kind of fasting, get the okay of your holistic physician to make sure you do not have any conditions that could make fasting dangerous for you.

Fasting is not recommended if you are an insulin-dependent diabetic; if you are on medications, or are being treated for an illness (unless the fasting is recommended by or supervised by your physician); or if you are pregnant.

When you have determined that it is safe for you to fast, you have a number of options to choose from. A detoxifying fast will increase the elimination of bodily wastes and thus benefit your body's healing mechanisms.

While you are fasting, however, your body will look upon itself as a source of fuel because you are not giving it its usual fuel, food. This means that you'll burn up fat tissue and muscle as fuel instead.

Research has shown that, although fasting is a quick way to rid the body of dangerous chemical toxins, such as those you may encounter by exposure to pesticides at a workplace or a toxic waste site, it can also be hazardous to detox in this way. Because fasting releases the toxins into your bloodstream so quickly and in great quantity, it may result in poisonous, toxic reactions that could be fatal. In all instances, *gradual* detoxification is best.

THE WATER FAST. In this short fast of up to three days, you consume only pure water, at least eight glasses each day. If you fast in this manner, take it easy for those days, since you will not be introducing any energy-producing substances into your body. Naps are recommended. Exercise is discouraged. Rest will enable your body to focus all of its attention on healing and eliminating. Fresh air, sunlight, and a good, long stretch in the morning and at night before going to bed will enhance your body's detoxification processes. You may choose to take a multivitamin and mineral supplement during this kind of fast, but do not take megadoses that you might take ordinarily on days when you are eating. A water fast can trigger the release of toxins into your bloodstream if you have high levels of toxins in your tissues (either accumulated or from a recent acute exposure), so if you even suspect that you may have a serious toxicity problem, do not fast.

When you break this fast, do so gently, by eating non-citrus fruit for breakfast on the first day after your fast. The high acid content in citrus fruits will irritate your empty stomach, so skip oranges, lemons, limes, grapefruit, and the like. For lunch that day eat fruit or a salad with a light dressing such as vinaigrette, but go easy on the vinegar when you prepare it, because it's acidic and could bother your stomach. For dinner, try a fruit salad or a green salad, and a cup of rice. Remember to drink plenty of water and as much fruit or vegetable juices as you'd like, throughout the day. You may want to skip the citrus fruit juices on this day, however, because of their acidity.

If you go on a water fast for more than two days (and never extend it past five days without medical supervision), your second day of solid food should resemble your first day. If your fast was for two days or less, your second day of eating should include fruits, vegetables, rice, pasta, other grains, nuts, and legumes, but very little meat or seafood.

THE WATER AND JUICE FAST. In this fast, you add fruit and vegetable juices to your water drinking. Drink approximately six glasses of pure water each day, plus moderate amounts of juice when you feel hungry or thirsty. The highly acidic citrus juices may bother an empty stomach, or you may do just fine during this fast because you are also consuming other non-acidic or low-acid juices, like carrot juice, pear juice, coconut milk, and homemade juices from raw vegetables of your choosing.

A water and juice fast can be chosen for a day, or for up to five days. It is not recommended to fast beyond that point without medical supervision. You may choose to take multivitamins and supplements while on this fast.

As with the water fast, you should take it easy, but since you are consuming fuel in the form of fruit and vegetable juices, your body is receiving energy, so you may be a bit more active than if you were on a water-only fast. Break the fast with the same diet that follows the water fast.

Even if you haven't been exposed to extreme toxicity, your body will be dumping accumulated toxins into your bloodstream when you fast. If you do not feel well while fasting, or experience anything other than mild, infrequent light-headedness, you should break the fast and detox more gradually by eating a light diet of fruits, vegetables, and grains for a week instead of fasting for a few days. Any questionable symptoms that arise, including heart palpitations, disorientation, extreme fatigue and weakness, shaking, fainting, or nausea may indicate an underlying disorder such as heart or blood sugar problems. Seek medical attention immediately.

If you experience a mild stomachache from citrus juices during a water and juice fast or from the total lack of food in a water fast, you may want to try drinking papaya juice. An enzyme present in this tasty tropical fruit helps aid digestion and soothe your stomach. If you experience any stomach upset during fasting, ginger tea—or pills—and watermelon can calm your stomach and relieve nausea.

You may also want to add herbal teas to either fast, especially echinacea tea, since this herb boosts the immune system.

24. Food Allergies, Sensitivities, and Intolerances

See chapter III, Environment, section 16. *In the Spotlight:* Allergies and Sensitivities.

In the Spotlight

25. Natural and Chemical Toxins in Food, Herbs, and Nutritional Supplements

A landmark study in 1981 reported the alarming news that about 35 percent of cancer deaths can be linked to carcinogens in foods. These include chemical toxins in foods, such as food additives and pesticides, and natural toxins, such as fungus.

A long-awaited follow-up analysis to assess the scope of the problem was published in February 1996 by the National Research Council in Washington, D.C. The 417-page report, "Carcinogens and Anti-Carcinogens in the Human Diet," cautions that there is still much we do not know regarding the interaction between the dozens—even hundreds—of chemical and natural toxins we consume each day and just how toxic each toxin may be. The report tries to be reassuring, by stating that "the great majority of individual naturally occurring and synthetic chemicals in the diet appears to be present at levels below which any significant adverse biologic effect is likely, and . . . are unlikely to pose an appreciable cancer risk."

But exactly what is "significant" and "appreciable"? If it happens to you, you'll certainly think your effects—the cancer—are "significant" and that your risk had been "appreciable." Is this just another way of playing with statistics in order to say, *Well, it happens, but the numbers aren't high enough or conclusive enough for us to call it a certain high risk?*

The report warns that "natural components of the diet may prove to be of greater concern" than the risks posed by chemical toxins, including pesticides, because natural toxins occur in higher numbers, are not regulated, or even sufficiently studied. Add these unknown risks to the many known risks of chemical toxins, and scientists realize we are in trouble and only beginning to scratch the surface.

Here are some of the things we *do* know:

TOXINS IN WATER: Among the sources of toxins in water, including drinking water, are:

- Human waste that leaks from septic tanks
- Toxic metals from ground water
- Toxic metals from water pipes
- Bacteria and viruses
- Toxic waste from industry and agriculture
- Animal waste in private and commercial farming areas
- Radioactive minerals
- Toxic by-products from the chlorine that disinfects our water supplies

Our water supplies are technically termed "disinfected," but plenty of toxins in varying amounts are still present.

FOOD ADDITIVES: Although they are listed on labels in some fashion, food additives can be difficult to understand. The flavor enhancer MSG (monosodium glutamate), for instance, often causes mild to severe reactions in people allergic or sensitive to it, but it can be disguised on a food label because it is often contained in other additives, such as hydrolyzed protein, and so is not required to be listed on its own as a separate ingredient. Other additives that commonly cause toxic reactions include sulfites and tartrazine (yellow dye #5).

IRRADIATION: The radiation of food to kill bacteria, insects, parasites, and to prolong shelf-life or slow down the ripening of fruits and vegetables is still a big safety question mark. Since we don't know yet the long-term effect of eating irradiated food, the safest thing to do is not buy it.

FOOD DYES: Skip foods with artificial colors, because chemical food dyes (but not natural ones made from vegetable and other nontoxic sources) can damage the immune system, damage DNA, increase cancer risk, and even speed up the aging process.

PRESERVATIVES: Natural preservatives, such as nutrients, citric acid, and ascorbic acid (forms of vitamin C) are safe, but chemical preservatives can be a problem. The aluminum compound alum, for example, used to put the crunch in pickled products, accumulates in the body and has toxic effects. So do other aluminum-based ingredients, including the aluminum salts in antacids and deodorants, and the aluminum in baking powder. You can avoid all this aluminum by buying brands of food and hygiene products in health food stores that are free of aluminum and other chemical preservatives.

ARTIFICIAL SWEETENERS: Saccharine and aspartame (Nutrasweet) have toxic effects, and even the natural sweetener sorbitol, if ingested in large amounts, can cause digestive distress and diarrhea. Use products sweetened by fruit juices, maple syrup, and other organics.

TOXINS IN COOKWARE: Bleached paper products (like coffee filters) have toxic dioxin residue. Aluminum cookware and food storage containers/bowls leech aluminum into your food, particularly foods that are acidic. Aluminum on the outside bottom of cookware is all right, since it doesn't come in contact with food. Microwaving food in plastic containers or in plastic wrap can result in plastic molecules contaminating your food. Stainless steel cookware contains nickel, which often produces an allergic reaction. Do not cook acidic foods (they release the nickel from the cookware into your food) in stainless steel. It's best to use glass cookware or cast iron. The amount of iron released from cast-iron cookware is not easily absorbed by your body, so unless you have a very high iron level, you will not suffer any toxic or unhealthy effects from using cast iron.

PESTICIDES AND FUNGICIDES: We have banned the use of certain pesticides in the United States, but we export those same pesticides to countries that use them on fruits and vegetables that are then imported into the United States and sold to unsuspecting American consumers. Therefore, stay away from produce from Mexico, South America, and Central America, which export produce to the United States that has been contaminated by these pesticides. Eat only organically grown produce that is pesticide- and fungicide-free. Many illegal pesticides are still being used in the United States, and the vegetables that are most affected by this include: hot peppers, green onions, blackberries, green peas, and pears. Again, if you eat only organic produce you'll avoid these problems.

Chemical Toxins in Meat, Poultry, Fish, Seafood, Eggs, and Milk Products

Animals destined to be on your plate are given lots of chemicals, hormones, and antibiotics. They are also exposed to environmental toxins and natural and chemical toxins in their feed. All of these toxins are then passed on to us when we dine on meat. Cooking all meat and poultry well, until it is no longer pink inside, will kill viruses and bacteria, but will not remove toxins and other kinds of contamination. You can, however, buy meat and poultry that has been raised completely free of chemicals, drugs, and hormones.

Fish and seafood are routinely contaminated by pesticide and sewage run-off and the water in which they live. Swordfish and tuna are routinely high in mercury. It is best to avoid all raw fish and seafood, which can also transmit diseases, such as hepatitis.

Eggs as well as poultry are routinely contaminated by salmonella and other bacteria. They need to be very well cooked to kill all bacteria, and you should never serve them on the same plates or with the same utensils used in their preparation, since those will contain raw juices that may be bacteria-contaminated. Be sure to clean all food-preparation surfaces immediately with bacteria-killing products.

Milk and milk products contain the toxic residue of the many drugs and hormones given regularly to dairy cows. Pasteurization does not rid the milk or milk products of these toxins. Try soy milk or rice milk as a substitute for animal milk.

Natural Toxins in Foods, Herbs, and Botanicals

Most, but not all, natural toxins are destroyed by cooking. These toxins commonly harm the immune system and cause illness as well.

- White mushrooms *(agaricus bisporus)*, the most common form found in grocery stores and on our tables, contain three natural toxins. Two are destroyed by cooking, but one is not. White mushrooms should not be eaten raw.
- Potatoes must be looked over carefully. Remove green parts of skin and all sprouts, since they are toxic.
- Peanuts and peanut butter can contain alfatoxin, a toxic mold.
- Alfalfa sprouts contain canavanine, which is a natural toxin. Forget any notion that these sprouts are a health food.
- Beans, peas, and all other legumes contain toxins that are killed by cooking.
- Peas are the only vegetable that contain lactose (milk sugar). While not a toxin, it can cause severe digestive disturbance if you are lactose intolerant.
- The sprouts of all legumes should not be eaten raw.
- Spinach, chard, and beet greens contain oxalic acid, which depletes your iron and calcium. Cook them lightly to deactivate the oxalic acid.
- Celery is fine eaten raw, as long as you remove all brown or pink patches, which are a toxic fungus.
- Cabbage, cauliflower, broccoli, kale, brussels sprouts, collard greens, mustard greens, and other cruciferous vegetables shouldn't be eaten in great quantities when raw, as they have a toxic effect and can cause stomach and intestinal distress.
- Squash and eggplant must be cooked well.

HEALING FOODS: Vegetables, fruits, and grains that are high in the antioxidants—vitamin C, E, and beta carotene—are particularly healing, and provide some of nature's most valuable preventives and antidotes. The high antioxidant vegetables include broccoli, brussels sprouts, carrots, cauliflower, oranges, orange juice, strawberries, and sweet potatoes.

The antioxidants are crucial to strengthening the immune system, preventing cancer, slowing the aging process, and protecting all of our systems from illness. Antioxidants protect us by neutralizing unstable, destructive oxygen molecules that destroy cells and consequently the tissues in our bodies. These nasty molecules are the free-radicals you've been hearing about so much in recent years.

Most fruits, vegetables, and grains are potentially healing, as long as they are cultivated safely and eaten properly—some should rarely, if ever, be eaten raw because of their natural toxins, as noted above.

Some plants, berries, mushrooms, and other foods that grow from the ground are simply poisonous all the time. Never eat anything in the wild that you cannot positively identify, and even then, think twice, unless, for example, they're the raspberries that grow wild at the edge of the meadow near your home and everyone has been eating them for decades and you know they're perfectly safe (and no one's been spraying them!).

Toxic Reactions to Herbs

Some herbs are too risky to take regularly, if at all.

- **Belladonna,** a stimulant and hallucinogen, causes an elevated heartbeat and has caused deaths in high doses.
- **Yohimbe,** used as a muscle builder and aphrodisiac, has caused psychotic reactions and fainting.
- **Black cohosh** and **blue cohosh,** commonly used to relieve menstrual pains, childbirth pains, and to induce labor or miscarriage. Regular use is not recommended since both have caused birth defects not only in laboratory animal studies, but also in livestock.

- **Senna,** a common ingredient in herbal weight-reducing or laxative teas and preparations, also used by itself for both purposes. Regular use can have disastrous effects, including loss of bowel function (the intestines and bowels eventually stop working because the senna has been doing their jobs for them). Fainting and intestinal pain is common with even short-term use. Senna has also been linked to heart attack deaths.

- **Sassafras,** used for centuries as a spring tonic, has caused liver cancer in lab rats when injected in high doses, and although it is now banned for use in food and drugs by the FDA (that's why you'll no longer find it as an ingredient in root beer), it is still available as an herb. The part of sassafras that is presumed a carcinogen is safrole, which is present in small concentrations only in the root bark of the plant. However, even with the safrole removed, rats given sassafras have developed liver cancer. In human studies, safrole did not metabolize into a carcinogen.

- **Pennyroyal** used in herbal preparations and alone as a way to bring on menstruation (and to induce a miscarriage as well) and is also used to cause perspiration during a cold or flu. The oil is used externally as a mosquito repellent and in animals as a flea repellant. Internal use of pennyroyal causes liver damage, internal bleeding, prevents clotting, and has been linked to a number of deaths. Although still sold in the United States, it is banned in Canada.

- **Chaparral** is hard to find these days, as many health stores will not carry it since the 1992 FDA warning against it. Commonly used as a blood purifier and to fight tumors, chaparral has caused liver damage in humans.

- **Lobelia** is used to treat asthma, bronchitis, coughs, and upper-respiratory illnesses because it provides bronchial dilation; it is also a fast-acting antispasmodic. A powerful emetic, just a few teaspoons of lobelia will bring on vomiting, and for that reason it has been used to treat food poisoning. With regular use and large doses, it is linked to toxicity and respiratory system paralysis.

- **Coltsfoot,** used to treat colds and coughs, has caused liver cancer in laboratory animals with regular use.
- **Kombucha tea,** actually a liquid culture made from the kombucha mushroom, has been the rage in recent years as a cure-all for everything from colds and wrinkles to cancer and AIDS. Toxicity is a major threat because of the fermentation process of this liquid fungus drink. It is typically made by individuals at home with no way to monitor the safety of the fermentation. It has been linked to toxic reaction and to two deaths by acidosis. The Centers for Disease Control (CDC) issued a warning in January 1996.
- **Comfrey** *(Symphytum officinale),* used for healing wounds, can be toxic to the liver, lungs, and other organs and should only be used externally.
- **Artemisia** (wormwood), used to treat fever, aches and pains, jaundice, hepatitis, and to kill worms and parasites, is linked to brain damage and death in humans, and has caused both in animal studies.
- **Goldenseal,** a popular cold and flu remedy, accumulates in your body and can result in toxic effects that include digestion problems, high blood pressure, and rapid heartbeat. It can be used safely by those who are not sensitive to it in small quantities, and not on a regular basis.
- **Ephedra,** a natural stimulant found in energy-boosting herbal formulas as well as herbal cold and flu remedies (its synthetic form, pseudophedrine, is a main ingredient in many over-the-counter cold, flu, asthma, and allergy drugs) can cause severe problems with regular use because it's such a powerful stimulant, including heart palpitations, heart irregularities, headache, insomnia, anxiety, nervousness, and circulation problems, and it

has been linked to several deaths. Ephedra is also known as the Chinese herb ma huang.

BEFORE USING ANY HERB, CONSULT A COMPLETE (RE-CENT, OR RECENTLY REVISED) REPUTABLE HERBAL GUIDE-BOOK THAT INCLUDES THE HERB'S MEDICINAL PROPERTIES, EFFECTS ON YOUR SYSTEMS, AND INTERACTIONS WITH OTHER SUBSTANCES. CONSULT WITH A HOLISTIC HEALTH CARE PRACTITIONER WITH HERBAL KNOWLEDGE IF YOU ARE IN NEED OF MORE INFORMATION. IF YOU SUSPECT YOU ARE PREGNANT, OR KNOW YOU ARE PREGNANT, DO NOT TAKE ANY HERBAL SUBSTANCES UNLESS THEY ARE OKAYED BY YOUR PHYSICIAN.

ALL HERBS CAN HAVE POTENTIALLY POTENT EFFECTS, ESPECIALLY WHEN USED IN IMPROPER DOSAGES OR OVER LONG PERIODS OF TIME. BE THOROUGHLY INFORMED BEFORE USING HERBS, BOTANICALS, OR ANY NUTRITIONAL SUPPLEMENTS.

In his comprehensive guide, *Natural Health, Natural Medicine,* alternative medicine pioneer Andrew Weil, M.D., reminds us that diet is the only major health component that is completely under our control.

His thorough presentation of the role of food, herbs, botanicals, supplements—basically, everything we ingest in the name of filling our stomachs or preserving health—has at its core the simple fact that the mainstream medical community is at long last coming around to: Healthy eating and eating habits activate the body's healing system.

But Dr. Weil cautions, as do other alternative medicine experts, that mainstream "nutritional science is primitive. Research on food and diet is much distorted by cultural biases and values, and the researchers are seldom able to see these distortions. There is no agreement from culture to culture on the answer to the most basic question of all: What is food, what is not?"

And, perhaps most important, he points out that "nutritional science gave us the Basic Four food groups, the concept responsible for much of our unhealthy obsession with protein. Registered dietitians are frequently witting or unwitting tools of the food industry, since the information they dispense often comes from industry rather than from disinterested sources."

In a most candid example, he summarizes the situation: "If you are tempted to follow their recommendations, remember that dietitians are the people responsible for the food served in schools and hospitals."

Toxicity and Vitamins, Minerals, and Nutritional Supplements

- **Antioxidants**—vitamins C, E, and beta carotene—combat what are known as the free-radicals in our bodies, which arise naturally or are produced by toxins and pollution. The free-radicals can cause cancer, heart disease, accelerate aging, and are suspected in a variety of other conditions. Although you can take more than 2,000 mg. of vitamin C every day and be relatively safe (you'll quickly excrete in your urine what your body doesn't absorb unless you take ridiculously high dosages), you should not overdo the other two antioxidants or you will feel fatigued and suffer muscle weakness. It's recommended that unless you are deficient in E and beta carotene and are being treated with larger doses by your holistic health care practitioner or physician for a particular reason, you should not exceed 400 I.U. of vitamin E per day, and 25,000 I.U. of beta carotene every other day. It is recommended that you take daily 2,000 mg. of Ester C (a type of vitamin C that isn't highly acidic and won't upset your stomach, and is also better absorbed than regular vitamin C), unless higher doses are necessary to treat cold, flu, or other conditions. You don't want to deactivate all of your free-radicals, as some are needed for normal energy production.
- **Vitamin A** is toxic in large doses, since it's fat soluble and stored in the body, not regularly excreted. An overdose can cause vomiting, joint pain, abdominal pain, itching, mood swings, headache, and severe liver damage. The RDA (recommended daily allowance) is 5,000 I.U.; you can overdose

by taking 25,000 I.U. per day over a period of weeks to several months.

- **Vitamin D** is toxic in large doses. The RDA is 400 I.U. per day, and it takes only 2,000 I.U. in a day to suffer toxic effects, which include liver damage, kidney disease, and increased risk of heart disease. The cholesterol in your skin produces natural vitamin D whenever you go out in the sun, and packaged foods are enriched with it, so unless you are diagnosed with a severe D deficiency, you won't need any more than the RDA of 400 I.U. per day.

- **Iron** can be a problem if it's too low, resulting in iron-deficiency anemia, characterized by a low red blood cell count. A shortage of red blood cells results in the blood being unable to carry enough oxygen to all parts of the body. Common symptoms include pale skin, fatigue, lethargy, dizziness, shortness of breath, rapid heart rate, loss of appetite, faintness, and ringing in the ears. Severe anemia may produce swollen ankles; rapid, weak pulse; clammy skin; and a feeling of fullness in the abdomen or neck. Too much iron, on the other hand, can cause a condition commonly referred to as "iron overload." The condition is rare, but can cause serious effects, including heart problems. Those with iron overload usually reduce their iron content a number of times per year by having blood withdrawn. Taking high doses of iron in supplements can cause constipation, diarrhea, and stomach distress.

- **Zinc** in high amounts can suppress your immune response and aggravate Alzheimer's disease.

- **Chromium, copper, and selenium** should be taken only in the amounts prescribed as the daily RDA, unless you are deficient, since these minerals can be toxic in large doses.

- **Calcium** deficiency may cause brittle bones, osteoporosis, and tooth problems. Exceedingly high doses of calcium can be toxic.

- **Niacin (vitamin B-3)** in high doses can cause liver problems and produce toxicity. Taking more than 1,000 mg. per day is enough to cause trouble.

- **Pryidoxine (vitamin B-6)** in doses higher than 300 mg. per day can cause nerve damage.
- **Vitamin K** can be toxic in high doses, as it is fat soluble and accumulates in the body. Do not take supplements beyond the daily RDA unless directed to do so for a deficiency diagnosed by your physician.

In short, do not arbitrarily take megadoses of *anything*. Consult with your physician or holistic health care practitioner if you suspect deficiencies or excesses of any nutrients.

VI

Illness, Injury, and Healing

26. Medications

All medications—natural, over-the-counter, prescription, and illegal/recreational—are potentially toxic. Toxicity can occur if medications are used in incorrect dosages; with substances with which they chemically interact; if they are used for too long; if they trigger an allergic or sensitivity reaction; if they cannot be tolerated by your systems; or if they are inherently toxic. Even the mercury in our dental fillings can be toxic.

In the interest of healing, we all too often become human laboratory experiments: Our mainstream physicians treat our symptoms, but rarely the underlying cause of our condition, by pumping us full of the prescription and over-the-counter pharmaceuticals the drug companies have been pushing. We become human toxic waste dumps from all the synthetic drug chemicals swirling about in our systems, causing side effects and weakening our healing mechanisms to the point where we become ill from what was supposed to help us heal in the first place.

Doctors' offices and hospitals are filled with people whose conditions have been directly caused by pharmaceutical drugs. Our society is also at fault. We have been conditioned to want the quick fix: a pill that we hope will make us feel better, whether or not it's actually helping our bodies heal, or even at the risk of its doing us more harm.

Drug addiction must be dealt with by holistic health care practitioners who specialize in addiction. The detoxification process must be supervised, and the All-Purpose Antidotes (described at the beginning of Part Three) can and should be incorporated into treatment.

Prevention

You must educate yourself regarding every medication you take. I highly recommend *The Pill Book: The Illustrated Guide to the Most-Prescribed Drugs in the United States* (Bantam), which is revised and updated every couple of years and is now in its sixth edition. This nearly 1,000-page paperback (priced at under $10 and available at bookstores as well as pharmacies) is the most thorough guide I've seen, of the several that are on the market. Read about each medication your doctor prescribes *before you even fill the prescription.* You may discover facts about the medication that make it undesirable. You are not some generic human—there is no such thing. You are unique, and you know your body better than your doctor does. While a particular medication may be fine for one person, it may not be for *you.* If you have any reservations about taking a drug that has been prescribed for you, discuss them immediately with your doctor and ask about the possibility of taking another, more appropriate medication, for you, or in some cases no drug at all, or getting an alternative treatment instead.

Before taking a medication (whether it's natural/herbal, over-the-counter, or prescription), if you are currently or have recently been on another medication or more, make sure that there will be no harmful interactions in your body between the drugs. Many medications also interact with foods, vitamins, nutrition supplements, and alcohol.

If you are going to use herbal or natural medications, consult with a thorough, reputable guidebook and remember that the effects on your systems of natural products are to be taken as seriously as pharmaceutical medications.

Follow all instructions and precautions regarding *all* the medications you take, whether they are pharmaceutical or natural.

If you are allergic, sensitive to, or have any kind of uncomfortable or harmful reaction to the substances commonly used as fillers in prescription, over-the-counter, or natural products—fillers include lactose (milk sugar), other milk products or by-products, corn, yeast, wheat, and eggs—tell your doctor to request medications that are free of these and any other kinds of fillers. Read labels carefully when purchasing over-the-counter or natural products. You now can find many that are free of these fillers, which will be noted on the label.

Antidotes

As long as they do not negatively interact with any medications you are taking, use the All-Purpose Antidotes to help detox your system from past or current use of medications. If you are on medication(s), check with your holistic health care practitioner or pharmacist before using *any* antidotes. Even when you are on medications, you can safely drink your eight glasses of pure water each day and eat your vegetables for fiber intake (both insure regular elimination of wastes and toxins), although timing may be a factor. Some medications should be taken with food, some on an empty stomach. Always check first in your pill book or other pharmaceutical reference, and your herbal and natural medicine guides as well, when you are considering using antidotes, and share this information with your physician, pharmacist, or holistic health care practitioner. Gentle, detoxing teas like Oriental Black Soybean Tea and Oriental Radish Tea (see the All-Purpose Antidotes), moderate exercise, meditation, dandelion root tea or capsules, Ester C, lymphatic drainage and other forms of massage are generally ideal for detoxing from medications and strengthening your healing mechanisms. But, again, before using any antidote that is internal, check with your holistic experts and in reputable published journals and books.

27. Fluid Retention

Caused by a seemingly infinite variety of factors, fluid retention has taken on seemingly epidemic proportions. It would appear that almost everyone has some kind of problem with it: puffy eyes; swollen legs or ankles; bloating; and swollen, sluggish, or clogged lymph glands.

Many medications cause or contribute to fluid retention and swelling. Too much salt in your diet can have these effects, too. Various illnesses and infections can cause swelling. So can digestive, intestinal, and elimination problems. Perhaps the most common factor involved with fluid retention and swelling, no matter where it is in your body, is poor lymphatic drainage.

The lymph glands exist to drain your tissues and systems, and they are crucial to removing all wastes and toxins from your body. Look at it this way: Your body is like a flowing river. Imagine that your lymph glands are big pipes, open at each end, that are as wide as the river, and placed at strategic points in this river. If the pipes are clear, the water can flow freely through them. If the pipes are clogged to any degree, the water will not get through in the constant, free-flowing way it needs to travel. The result is stagnated water that becomes toxic. It cannot pass in sufficient quantities through the pipe to continue its journey out the other side to the next part of the river.

Lymphatic drainage massage helps to clear the lymph glands (the big pipes in the river), so fluid can flow freely and toxins and waste can continue on their path to elimination via urine, feces, perspiration, and breath.

Prevention

Lymphatic drainage massage on a regular basis can help prevent most problems with fluid retention and swelling. You can either massage yourself in the shower, using your soapy hands, or at any time using body lotion. A partner can massage you, too, but you should have a professional treatment from time to time as well, especially if you have any fluid retention in your body or dark circles or discoloration around your eyes. Massage all the lymph glands in your body (see the section on the immune system in Part One for locations of the lymph glands and a thorough explanation of the lymph system) for a few minutes each day to help prevent swelling in your body and sluggish or clogged lymph drainage. Drink plenty of pure water to help flush out the toxins that need to be released.

Antidotes

Lymphatic drainage massage is also the antidote, of course. Do you have clogged sinuses? Massage the lymph glands on either side of your neck, just below each ear, and under your jaw just above your neck. Once these glands are cleared, all fluids from the face will have an open door and be able to drain freely. Massaging these neck glands will also get rid of puffy eyes, dark circles, or dark skin around your eyes and help drain the nose and ears. For ears, you should massage the area in front of your ear where it meets your head; under your ear, behind the lobe, where the ear meets the neck; and everywhere your ear is attached to your head.

You also should massage the areas between the nearest gland and the swollen or affected area. For example, if the problem is swollen feet, you need not only to massage the glands on either side of your groin, but also to massage your ankles, calves, knees (front and back), and thighs, as the area between the lymph glands in the groin area and your swollen ankles is the pathway for the fluid's travels.

Massage deeply the lymph glands under each arm and the area next to them on the side of the breast area, as well as the glands in your chest, on the left and the right, just below the collarbone, for drainage of the entire upper body, including the head. (Women, see chapter IV, The Female Body, section 17, Breasts, for more on upper body lymphatic drainage.)

Drink a glass or two of pure water after doing lymphatic drainage massage to help flush out your systems.

Herbs with a mild diuretic effect are also excellent at detoxing, such as dandelion root in tea or capsule form, and will help enhance the process of draining your systems. But remember to rehydrate by drinking at least eight glasses of pure water each day.

Once you've begun clearing out and opening up your drainage systems, you will notice improvement and feel better quickly. Draining the facial tissues gives results in minutes. Over the course of hours, days, or weeks, you will see enormous improvement in all areas of your body. Lymphatic massage will also greatly improve your circulation, reduce the effects of stress, help you clear out emotional debris, and have an overall relaxing effect.

Using any of the All-Purpose Antidotes listed at the opening of Part Three in conjunction with lymphatic drainage, helps support the draining, detoxing, and healing processes, and they are highly recommended.

28. Lack of Sleep

Your body, mind, and spirit are done great harm by consistent lack of sleep or sleep deprivation. Lack of sleep interferes with your body's healing mechanisms, your immune system—your entire physical, emotional, and spiritual well-being.

If your sleep is interrupted or inadequate because you are a new mother (or new father), read section 20 of chapter IV, The Female Body. If your lack of sleep is due to stress and/or a busy schedule that leave you with little time for sleep, read all of the sections in chapter II, Emotional and Spiritual Stress, since those preventive measures and antidotes will help you deal not only with the sleep issue, but the larger ones that cause or affect it.

If the problem stems from illness or reaction to medications, consult with your holistic health care practitioner and physician, but use caution when presented with the option of any kind of pharmaceutical sleeping pill—they are habit-forming, addictive, and come with lots of toxic side effects. Try natural, relaxing, sleep-inducing remedies instead.

Prevention

Get to the root of your sleep problem and treat the problem. If the problem is that you are not giving yourself enough time for adequate sleep, change that situation immediately. Adequate sleep is not some optional luxury. It is a necessity. You probably don't need anyone to tell you how toxic lack of sleep is to your entire being—you already know that because you feel lousy. Now you have to do something about it. Make finding that extra time for sleep your number one priority, because your lack of sleep is the catalyst for so much of whatever else is troubling you physically and/or emotionally. Most adults need between six and eight hours of sleep each night, minimum, to facilitate health and well-being. Everyone is different, however. Maybe you do very well on less, maybe you need more. If you are not feeling well on the amount of sleep you are currently getting, you know better than anyone that you need more pillow time.

If you work during evening hours, or in a combination of day and evening shifts, a healthy sleep schedule will be even more difficult to maintain.

To help you relax and ease into sleep, drink calming herbal teas, such as chamomile, but *do not* use alcohol or drugs to wind down and induce sleepiness. Take a warm/hot shower and wash slowly, almost meditatively, with your eyes closed. Take a bubble bath, or a bath with calming essential oils, such as lavender, sandalwood, clarysage, geranium, lemon, chamomile, rose, hyacinth, jasmine, carnation, jonquil, or vanilla.

If someone else is there with you at bedtime, have him or her give you a relaxing massage from head to toe. After that, you'll probably drift off instantly.

Before bedtime is an ideal time to meditate, which will also help you clear the stresses of the day out of your system. Try a variety of meditative experiences: eyes open, eyes closed, with soothing music, in silence, gazing at the night sky, whatever helps put you in a meditative state.

Antidotes

The preventive suggestions are antidotes to being wide awake. To help restore your health when lack of sleep has taken its toll, follow the All-Purpose Antidotes at the beginning of Part Three, and add as many relaxing detoxing practices to your schedule as you can. These include exercise (which actually makes it easier for you to fall asleep at bedtime, even if your exercise was in the morning), meditation, bodywork and massage, and the spiritual practices of your choice.

29. Injury

When healing from an injury, you are faced with a number of potentially toxic situations: an accumulation of fluids (see section 27, Fluid Retention), the effects of medications (see section 26, Medications), emotional healing (see chapter II, Emotional and Spiritual Stress), and, of course, the injury itself.

Prevention

When it comes to injury, what preventive words can there be except for "Be careful next time!" In terms of having the optimum conditions for healing after an injury, one rule always applies: the healthier you were and the stronger your immune system was before the injury, the better off you'll be during and after the injury when your body, mind, and spirit are all on red alert, activating all your healing processes.

Antidotes

The All-Purpose Antidotes presented at the beginning of Part Three play dual roles as detoxing and healing treatments when you are recuperating from injury. Remember, though, to check with your holistic physician before using any of them (except for the recommendation to meditate, drink eight glasses of pure water each day, and eat enough fiber) to make sure the antidotes will not interact in a harmful way with any medications you may be taking.

To relieve the aches and pains that accompany sprains; muscle or tendon strains, pulls, or injuries; bruises and physical overexertion, a simple hot springs bath at home works wonders to detoxify and promote healing. Add three tablespoons of baking soda to your bathwater. Soak for 15 minutes, and don't rinse. This bath detoxes, soothes muscles, relieves aches and pains, stimulates your circulation, relaxes you, and as a nice bonus, it also softens your skin. Enjoy one of these baths as often as you'd like; it's good for all skin types.

As long as none of its ingredients interfere with any medications you might be taking, try this massage for the same kind of injuries for which the hot springs bath is recommended. To one tablespoon of a neutral lotion or cream base (like Vaseline Intensive Care or Eucerin cream), add the following essential oils: 5 drops of eucalyptus, 5 drops of peppermint, 5 drops of ginger. Rub or massage as needed. The mixture will relieve soreness and sore muscles; neutralize lactic acid, which makes overworked muscles hurt; stimulate circulation, which is vital for healing; and help eliminate toxins and wastes.

If your injuries involve broken bones, wounds, surgery, stitches, or any invasive procedures, check with your holistic physician before using any of the antidotes, with the exception of pure water and meditation. If you receive the go-ahead, antidotes that will be helpful for elimination of toxins and promotion of healing in these circumstances include those outlined in the All-Purpose Antidotes, and others, particularly dandelion root tea or pills/capsules, echinacea to boost the immune system, the antioxidant vitamins, vibrational medicine (particularly the Bach Flower Remedies' Rescue Remedy, acupuncture, acupressure, light therapy, music and sound therapy), and lymphatic drainage massage. Your health care practitioners may also recommend various hydrotherapy procedures (physical therapy in specialized tubs of water) under the supervision of a trained specialist.

30. Illness

What is an illness? This rather vague term is applied to everything from not feeling well to a terminal disease. How do we prevent and treat any form of illness, no matter if it's minor or major? Surprisingly, in a very similar manner, as all disorders of the body can stem from toxic action.

Prevention and Antidotes

In addition to the All-Purpose Antidotes and all the other health-giving methods mentioned in this book, bodywork and massage treatments stand out as ideal preventive and treatment measures. They detox the body, mind, and spirit, and promote healing for all illnesses.

By directly stimulating your body's systems, all forms of massage and bodywork are valuable tools for literally helping your body clear its toxins and toxic accumulation of your body's natural substances. Massage focuses on the body's muscles and tissues; specialty massages also stimulate circulation and help clear and realign your body's flow of energy. Bodywork treatments combine massage techniques with other hands-on techniques not strictly classified as massage because they focus on other components of your body, not just your muscles and tissues.

The Seymour System, for example, developed by Miami-based Gladys Seymour Davis, focuses on detoxifying and contouring the entire body, as well as jump-starting the lymphatic, circulatory, and other vital systems. The idea behind this and other bodywork treatments is to free up the fat, excess fluids, and toxins so the body can process and then eliminate them and heal itself. Using the bones in her hands, in effect turning the sides of the thumbs and fingers into sculpting tools, Davis works on the body in up-and-down movements (not circular, like massage), following the acupuncture and acupressure meridian lines of Chinese Medicine. These lines are like the seams of the body and represent the pathways that energy takes through the body, according to Chinese Medicine.

You can work on your own body using these same methods to stimulate your body's systems, including the lymphatic system. Deeply "pump out" each of the lymph glands: on either side of the neck, under the jawline, under each arm, in the chest, and where the thigh meets the torso near the groin area. These lymph areas become routinely clogged and keep the body from flushing out properly, leading to puffiness, swelling, impaired immune system functions and disease-fighting capabilities, and a whole host of other systemic problems. Accumulated toxins in the tissue spaces and muscles are also released in the process of pumping out the lymph glands.

Treating the body in this manner also includes paying particular attention to the joints, which become partly clogged by fatty deposits.

You can give yourself bodywork treatments on a daily basis while you use soap in the shower or body lotion afterward, and visit a bodywork or massage therapist for more complete treatments periodically. Not only does an overall treatment, such as the Seymour System developed by Davis, keep all your systems running and detoxing smoothly, it also helps remove fatty deposits.

Bodywork and massage treatments should not be used if you have or have had cancer unless your physician says that you are free of cancer cells, because malignant cells can spread through your body as a result of these techniques.

Bodywork also increases your energy and greatly benefits your mind and spirit. It helps release pent-up or buried emotions and reduces not only stress but the physical and emotional effects of stress.

Results of bodywork are felt quickly. These include relief from pain, elimination of swelling, improved circulation, relaxed muscles, improved skin tone, a healthier immune system and therefore increased resistance to illness, smoother joint movements, fewer fat deposits, more physical energy, improved emotional outlook, and greater ease of motion overall.

If you haven't already read section 17, Breasts, in chapter IV, The Female Body, go back and do it now, even if you are a man. The lymphatic drainage principles and the bra/constrictive clothing problem discussed there represent important prevention and antidote issues for both men and women. These areas were first linked by naturopath and lymphologist Marika Von Viczay, N.D., Ph.D. in the early 1970s. A natural healing and detoxification pioneer, Dr. Von Viczay is the director of the ISIS Health and Rejuvenation Center in Asheville, North Carolina, and a consultant at the Health Regeneration Institute, a complementary medicine center in Waynesville, North Carolina, where she treats not only "whatever ails you" but has developed specialized cancer prevention, healing, and detoxification programs.

Dr. Von Viczay teaches patients that when lymphatic circulation slows down, your systems become toxic, and cancer can develop. Muscle tension, stress, and inactivity also contribute to the impairment of your lymph fluid flow. As a result, toxins and protein accumulate in the lymph vessels and nodes, which then become clogged and inflamed. The fluid thickens, and your systems become toxic and oxygen-deprived. Not only cancer but other serious degenerative disorders can develop. To prevent, heal, and detox, you need to rid your body of lymph congestion, clearing out the waste debris, toxins, and fatty acids that the lymph system is designed to filter and eliminate from the body.

Dr. Von Viczay focuses her work on these processes, and in addition to hands-on lymphatic drainage massage, she recommends Electro-Lymphatic Therapy (ELT), which she created in the 1980s when she discovered that light emissions can unclog the lymphatic system. (This is yet another of the growing number of conditions that respond to the healing use of light; see the entry on light therapy in the Vibrational Medicine section of Part Two, Natural Treatments.) Lymph congestion is cleared, reduced, and dispersed in response to a particular frequency of light emission.

For cancer patients (and those with AIDS-related cancer) Dr. Von Viczay recommends jumping on a trampoline for no more than a total of 15 minutes every day. The anti-gravity effect causes lymph fluid to flow upward, helping to unclog and detox the lymph glands. She does not recommend hands-on lymphatic drainage massage for cancer patients, because dispersing lymph fluid in that manner increases the risk of spreading cancer cells through the lymph system. The trampoline exercise prompts lymph clearing and detoxification without the risk of pumping cancer cells through the systems.

Dr. Von Viczay's treatment for cancer and many other conditions includes a nutrition, supplement and herbal program, focusing on a diet containing a lot of cooked vegetables and spirulina (blue-green algae in powder or capsules), the use of immune-enhancing nutrients, and mind-body relaxation. Many cancer patients who follow her lymphatic treatment total program avoid lymph node removal (a surgery commonly recommended by physicians treating breast cancer and other cancer patients, either as a preventive measure or because cancer cells have invaded the lymph nodes). Her treatments have resulted in a 70 to 80 percent cure rate for early stage cancers.

The comprehensive treatments created by Gladys Seymour Davis and Marika Von Viczay show how all of your systems interact and just how important preventive measures are. Prevention means not only preventing illness, disease, and "whatever ails you" but preventing the situations that set the stage for those unhealthy conditions. This usually means employing natural methods to keep your systems running unimpaired; lowering your exposure to toxins; eating a balanced, healthy, low-fat diet free of processed and chemically enhanced foods and full of organic, natural foods; getting daily exercise, sun, and fresh air; and dealing with emotions before they are suppressed and manifest as physical illness. Add to this the spiritual components of making choices that lead you toward an empowered, fulfilled life, doing what you came here to do. This involves an awareness of your interconnectedness with everything in the universe, including an innate creative source—and therefore your natural ability to create the life you want—and an awareness of the true nature of yourself as a spiritual being who is essentially just having a human experience.

Getting into the specifics of preventing illness, disease, and "whatever ails you" first requires you to know exactly who you are physically, emotionally, and spiritually. Only then can you know how to prevent and treat toxic situations. There are plenty of natural health practitioners to help you put all of this together, but you can do so much of it on your own with the help of the amazing array of information now available in print, audio, video, on the Internet, in lectures, and workshops.

Your first step should be to take advantage of one of the good components of modern mainstream medicine: diagnostic tests. Before you can really begin prevention, you have to know what you're dealing with. Complete blood tests and urinalysis will show, among dozens of other things, whether you have any vitamin or other nutrient deficiencies; anemia or other underlying conditions; immune system problems; hormone imbalances; illnesses, diseases, or factors that may show you are at risk, on the verge of, or in the early stages of an imbalanced, unhealthy, or toxic condition, hereditary condition, or anything else that can spell trouble. For more on this, see chapter X, Times of Life, section 50, *In the Spotlight:* Annual Physicals Timeline.

You'll also want to have other diagnostic tests done, not only if you suspect a problem, but just to see what's going on in there (especially if you've never had any of them). If you're a woman, tests might include a breast sonogram (mammograms routinely miss things, especially if you have low-fat breasts) and a sonogram of the pelvic area that can show any problems with the reproductive system, including uterine fibroids, endometriosis, ovarian cysts, tumors, and other conditions you may not be aware you have in the absence of any noticeable symptoms. If you're a man, you'll want to have the PSA blood test for prostate cancer. If you've been a smoker for many years, a chest X ray and other diagnostic tests can alert you to the earliest stages of lung problems.

To both prevent and treat the toxic situations that accompany "whatever ails you" and the healing process, see other sections in this book that may apply to your particular condition, including chapter II, Emotional and Spiritual Stress, and section 26, Medications, in this chapter. You can cross reference every part of this book in order to help you deal with detoxing during any illness and during healing.

Before you use any of the All-Purpose Antidotes (listed at the opening of Part Three) or other preventive or antidote measures in this book, remember to check with your holistic physician or health care practitioner if you are pregnant, on medication(s), or are being treated for any condition.

You may find that going in one particular healing direction is appealing, and that may mean working with Ayurvedic or Chinese Medicine physicians and practitioners, for example, or by combining a variety of approaches under the care of a naturopathic physician (N.D.), holistic M.D., or other natural practitioner. You'll find a list of organizations that can help you find these kinds of physicians and health care practitioners at the end of the book, in Resources.

Perhaps the most toxic of ailments is cancer (and AIDS-related cancer), not only because of its devastating effects but because of the highly toxic nature of its mainstream treatments, chemotherapy and radiation. You may want to use natural/alternative methods to treat cancer, under the guidance of a naturopathic or holistic doctor and other practitioner, because mainstream treatments will weaken you with their toxic effects. Often you hear of patients who successfully treated and cured cancer (even in later stages) with natural medicine approaches (including detoxification, dietary changes, vitamins, herbs, supplements, vibrational medicine, you name it) and limited, if any, mainstream approaches. In fact, a University of Illinois Medical School study shows many patients who have taken alternative approaches to be cancer-free and/or living many years beyond doctors' predictions.

However, if you opt for the aggressive mainstream approaches first, you will be greatly weakening an already frail, cancer-ridden body, the studies show. Death rates climb when mainstream treatments alone are used, or when natural treatments are put off until the body has been so damaged by both the cancer and the chemo and radiation that nothing could possibly help.

Long-term AIDS survivors have most often relied heavily on natural treatments and mind-body medicine. You hear about patients who have exhausted the mainstream treatments and, close to death, finally turn to natural treatments. Sometimes, a patient miraculously rebounds in this kind of scenario, but most often it's too late. The overwhelming toxic damage done by chemotherapy and radiation prove to be too much for any kind of natural (or mainstream, for that matter) treatment to make much of a difference. Given all this chemo and radiation, you'd think we were progressing in cancer treatment, but when using these mainstream toxic treatments, the five-year survival rates for cancers of the liver, lungs, pancreas, bone, and breast haven't improved one bit in the last twenty-five years.

More than 50 percent of cancer patients now seek alternative treatments, various polls show. Researchers and mainstream physicians are even looking more and more toward alternative, natural treatments, and realizing that by strengthening the cancer patient's body, you improve greatly your chances of fighting the cancer. The mainstream is now incorporating the use of food, nutrients, vitamins and supplements, exercise, yoga and meditation and other stress-reduction techniques, visualization, expressing and releasing emotions, positive outlook and humor into mainstream cancer treatment.

AIDS

Studies show that the majority of AIDS patients seek alternative treatments, and research has indicated that any alternative treatment that boosts the immune system can greatly help AIDS patients' severely depleted immunity. A recent study conducted by the Touch Research Institute at the University of Miami School of Medicine revealed that immunity was increased among AIDS patients who receive daily massages.

The use of effective immune system–boosting herbs such as echinacea is also recommended by the medical community. Dosage should be determined by your holistic health care practitioner based upon your individual needs.

Detoxification is an important component in the treatment of AIDS-related illnesses. The immune system is so impaired that the body can't adequately detox itself, and the toxins introduced into the body in the form of chemotherapy is literally poison to the body, which is why it can kill cancer cells.

Use all of the All-Purpose Antidotes in the treatment of AIDS-related illnesses, with the approval of your physician. Any other preventive methods and antidotes discussed in this book can also be used in those particular situations, again with the approval of your physician.

In the Spotlight

31. Cold and Flu

Adverse side effects are among the top three consumer complaints about modern cold medicines. They can make you drowsy, restless, or hyperactive; they interact with other medications you might be taking, causing even more serious complications. Pharmaceutical cold medicines can also do you more harm than good because, in an attempt to control the symptoms of cold and flu, they interfere with the body's healthy detox actions: all that mucus is your body's way of detoxing—of ridding itself of infection. You don't want to dry it up; you want to help your body get rid of even more of it.

Of course, cold symptoms are mighty uncomfortable. You can ease some of them with natural treatments and herbal preparations that won't interfere with your body's healthy detoxing action. These natural treatments will also address the illness itself. Symptoms are actually the body's effort to reestablish balance, so use products, substances, and therapies that support rather than suppress the body's inherent efforts to heal itself.

Homeopathic remedies, for example, help relieve symptoms and strengthen the body so that the symptoms don't return as frequently or as severely. Free of side effects, noninteractive with drugs, and nontoxic, natural remedies containing herbs, botanicals, vitamins, and minerals are also ideal when treating children. Homeopathic medicines are available over-the-counter at natural food and health stores, and are regulated by the Food and Drug Administration (FDA).

Natural remedies are botanical and mineral in their purest form, contain no artificial colors or flavors, no animal by-products, or products that commonly cause an allergic reaction or a food-sensitive reaction, such as fillers like yeast, corn, wheat, or lactose. Many natural remedies are available that combine a number of herbs, botanicals, and nutrients. You can take preparations that include a combination of botanicals, or take them individually.

One of the most effective cold and flu treatments is the anti-infective, immune system-boosting herb echinacea. Also known as the purple coneflower, this plant resembles the black-eyed Susan, but with a purple center and daisylike petals. Native Americans used echinacea more than any other as prevention and treatment for a broad range of conditions and situations.

Two species, *Echinacea angustifolia* and *Echinacea purpurea,* are the primary varieties used for healing, though *angustifolia* is by far the most effective. You'll more often find the *purpurea* species alone or in combination with *angustifolia* in teas, tinctures, capsules, and other preparations, chiefly because *purpurea* is inexpensive (which is not to say that *angustifolia* is expensive—it isn't). However, herbalists and physicians recommend sticking with *angustifolia* alone, because it so outshines its sister species.

As a highly effective immune system booster, echinacea strengthens your body's natural infection-fighting capabilities. It also works quickly, with no side effects, and can be given to children. *In fact, if taken at the first sign of a cold or the flu, echinacea will stop an infection in its tracks.*

Here's how: Take half of a dropper of echinacea liquid if you are a child or an adult weighing 110 pounds or less, or 1 dropperful if you weigh more than 110 pounds, in a cup of any liquid as soon as possible after your symptoms begin. Continue the dosage every four hours. No need to wake up in the middle of the night for a dosage, however—your body needs rest, so take your dosage when you wake up in the morning.

If you've caught the cold or flu in time, you should be able to ward off the full-fledged version within 12 to 18 hours of your first echinacea dosage. This works because echinacea strengthens your body's immune response, so your body's natural defense system is getting rid of the bug. If your symptoms do disappear after 12 to 18 hours, stay on the echinacea dosage cycle for another two days. If your symptoms do not go away after that initial period, all is not lost. Stay on the echinacea dosage cycle for the duration of your cold or flu. Your symptoms will be milder than they would have been if you weren't taking echinacea, and the duration of your illness will be shorter, perhaps only half as long as you would have been ill otherwise. Once your symptoms are gone, stay on the echinacea dosage cycle for another three days.

If you're reading this with a cold or flu, start taking echinacea right away, every four hours, for the duration of your illness.

Liquid echinacea (called a tincture) is the most effective form. Most brands do not need refrigeration, as they are preserved in a miniscule amount of alcohol (so little you'll never feel it; a far smaller ratio than what's in over-the-counter cough medicines), so it's easy to carry it with you when you're not at home. Remember to use only the *angustifolia* species, and to use only 100 percent echinacea, not echinacea in combination with other herbs, like goldenseal, which are common combinations. You want plain old full-strength echinacea; if you wish, you can take other herbal preparations separately.

A word of caution about goldenseal, which has become a popular ingredient in natural cold remedies. It can also be taken alone, but it accumulates in your systems, and since its most active component is hydrastine, which aids circulation, it will overstimulate the nervous system.

Echinacea will lose its effectiveness if it is overused because it is such a powerful immune system booster. You don't want to overboost the system, so it's suggested that you take at least five days off from echinacea before taking it again if you've been on it for more than a week. Many people like to take echinacea as a preventive during cold and flu season, or if they've been in contact with someone who is ill. This is an excellent idea; however, cycle your dosages this way if you are using it as a preventive: Take the dropper amount based on weight as directed earlier, once a day for seven days, then skip the next five days, then repeat the cycle as often as needed. If you've just been in contact with someone who may be contagious, or are in continuous contact (at home, work, or wherever), take echinacea twice a day, seven days on, then five days off.

Echinacea is an effective antibiotic, too, which is why it's been popular for centuries. It found its way from Native American healing practices into modern medicine in the 1920s, but was replaced in the 1930s with synthetic drugs that could be patented and made highly profitable. Now, however, it has made a huge comeback and pharmaceutical companies are looking for a way to profit off it as well as other natural healing botanicals.

Garlic has been used since pre-Biblical times by cultures around the world because of its superb ability to destroy or inhibit various bacteria, fungi, and yeasts. The component that does this—allicin— is also the one that gives garlic its strong odor, although you can get around that by taking odor-free garlic capsules, which neutralize garlic's odor without destroying the allicin. In the traditional medicine of China and Europe, garlic has long been used for respiratory ailments and has proved effective in treating cold and flu symptoms while killing bacteria and virus, stimulating the immune system, and healing the lungs. During the seventeenth century, survivors of the Plague credited garlic.

In 1858, Louis Pasteur noted garlic's antibacterial properties, and during World War I, garlic was in widespread use in hospitals as an antiseptic. Finally, in the 1940s, modern science was able to explain exactly how garlic worked as a medicine. Dr. Arthur Stoll, a Swiss chemist, extracted an oil from garlic and named it alliin, then discovered a garlic enzyme he named aminase. This enzyme changes the alliin oil into garlic's active healing ingredient allicin when garlic is cut or crushed. Even when allicin is diluted with water to 1/120,000, it is still able to kill the germs that cause cholera and typhoid fever. Allicin also acts as an effective oxidizer and a strong disinfectant.

For garlic's medicinal properties to be most effective, it is recommended that you eat the fresh clove, uncooked, as heating destroys the allicin. It is also slowly destroyed by aging, although it takes nearly two years for all of the allicin to be rendered inactive. Garlic can also kill staph and strep bacteria, some influenza viruses, and is more effective against typhus than penicillin.

For cold, flu, fever, and infectious diseases, fresh garlic juice, garlic oil, chopped uncooked garlic, garlic syrup, garlic tea, and garlic tincture are powerful remedies. Here are a few recipes and dosages:

GARLIC OIL: Place eight ounces of peeled, minced garlic in a jar with enough olive oil to cover. Close tightly and shake a few times each day; allow to stand in a warm place for three days. Press and strain it through an unbleached muslin or cotton cloth and store in a cool place. *Take one teaspoon every hour.*

GARLIC SYRUP: Place one pound of peeled, minced garlic in a two-quart jar and almost fill the jar with equal parts of apple cider vinegar and distilled water. Cover and let stand in a warm place for four days, shaking a few times a day. Add one cup of glycerine and let stand another day. Strain, and, with pressure, filter the mixture through a muslin or linen cloth. Add one cup of honey and stir until thoroughly mixed. Store in a cool place. *Take one tablespoon of garlic syrup three times a day before meals.*

GARLIC TEA: Chop several cloves of garlic and let soak in half a cup of water for six to eight hours. (Do not heat the water as you would do with conventional tea.) *Drink tea for symptoms of cold and flu, or gargle for a sore throat.*

GARLIC TINCTURE: Soak half a pound of peeled garlic cloves in one quart of brandy. Shake a few times each day. After two weeks, strain. *Take up to 25 drops a day as needed.* (Keeps for one year.)

Obviously, don't wait until you are actually sick to make these garlic preparations (with the exception of the tea). You may want to make them as soon as cold and flu season begins or when anyone you know becomes ill. Many of these preparations can also be found already made in your local natural health food store.

For clearing your nose and sinuses, open a jar of horseradish and take a big whiff. Look for natural teas, cough drops, and other preparations that contain eucalyptus, which helps clear mucus but is also an active germicide with antiseptic and astringent qualities. The oil is also an effective expectorant, which is why it's found in pharmaceutical as well as natural cough syrups.

Australian aborigines were probably the first to discover that the oil eucalyptol is a beneficial medicine. Eucalyptus has a spicy, almost minty, cool taste and refreshing smell, and it is also very effective as a steam inhalation to loosen mucus from the sinuses and lungs. Eucalyptus is quite powerful, so a little goes a long way.

STEAM INHALATIONS: Place two drops of eucalyptus essential oil in a medium-size pot of water and bring to a boil. Remove from heat. Place a towel over your head, tent style, and bend over the steaming pot of water. Do not place your face too close to the pot. Inhale and exhale for 5 to 10 minutes. You can do this seated at a table—and you can certainly come out of the tent for some cooler air once in awhile.

Another steam inhalation that works well because of the antibacterial and antiviral properties of the essential oils: Combine one drop each of thyme, tea tree oil, lavender, and clove. Follow the same procedure as above.

TISSUE INHALER: Carry a portable inhaling treatment with you by dabbing essential oils directly on a tissue or white cotton handkerchief. Inhale from it as needed to help relieve a stuffy nose and drain the sinuses, as well as unclog chest congestion. Use any of the essential oil combinations from the steam inhalation recipe, or try this one, a favorite of aromatherapists: Combine one drop each of red thyme, peppermint, eucalyptus, and clove.

DETOXING MASSAGE: Add one drop of lemon oil, two drops of eucalyptus, and three drops of rosemary to one teaspoon of vegetable oil, massage oil, or unmedicated moisturizing cream (Vaseline Intensive Care or Eucerin work well). Massage into your chest, neck, forehead, nose, and cheeks to relieve congestion and encourage drainage. For added benefit, inhale as you massage.

FEVER: A higher than normal temperature (above 98.6) is one of your body's ways of killing bacteria and viruses and expelling toxins through perspiration. Drinking warm teas and soups and piling on the blankets will help relieve the chills that often accompany a fever. To help break a fever, dip washcloths into ice water, wring out and place around the front and back of the neck and across the forehead.

LYMPHATIC DRAINAGE: To help drain the lymph glands on either side of your neck, stimulate circulation, and relieve a sore throat, try a grated carrot poultice. Grate carrot, place on a white handkerchief, fold edges in to make a flat poultice, and wrap another handkerchief around it to help keep the carrot from falling out. Now wrap the poultice around your throat, safety pin it in place, and take a lightweight dish towel that has been soaked in ice water and wrap it around the poultice, tying it in back. Keep the poultice on for 30 to 45 minutes, or until it becomes very warm. Repeat as often as needed.

SORE THROAT: Drink tea made from the herb slippery elm, also known as red elm. It's the active ingredient in many of the blends of herbs used in sore throat teas you'll find at the natural food store. Slippery elm soothes sore and irritated throats, helps with a dry throat, coughing, and lung congestion.

⌘ VII ⌘

Leisure, Exercise, and Sports

32. Lack of Exercise

*I*f you are leading a sedentary life, you put yourself at risk for many illnesses. You are also compromising the effectiveness of your body's systems and their ability to perform their detoxification functions.

Prevention

Before beginning any regular exercise program, get a complete physical, especially if you are overweight, in poor health, or have led a sendentary life for a number of years. Lack of exercise is toxic to your body. Exercise will bring healthy changes to you physically, emotionally, and spiritually, and it also will release stored toxins. It is therefore important to take steps to prevent the uncomfortable effects that might come with a long overdue release. One way to do that, of course, is to incorporate other healthy healing practices into your life, including healthy eating, bodywork, fresh air and sunshine, vitamins and other nutritional supplements, system-strengthening herbs, yoga, breathwork, meditation, and other relaxation/antistress techniques, lymphatic drainage massage (to eliminate stored toxins in the all-important lymph system), and drinking eight glasses of pure water each day to help flush out toxins quickly and consistently.

Antidotes

The antidote for the lack of exercise and physical activity is, of course, incorporating exercise and physical activity into your life. To facilitate healing and the release of long-stored toxins, use all of the

All-Purpose Antidotes; they will affect all of your systems when used together, in a gentle but effective and consistent way. You may want to consult with a holistic health care practitioner if it has been a long time since you've been active, and you'll definitely want to be under the supervision of a professional if you have been ill, are currently ill, or are healing from any condition that has required medication, surgery, or an extensive period of recuperation.

When returning to an exercise or beginning any new exercise, you may get sore muscles. See the next section on the subject of overexertion for soothing detoxing baths, body rubs, and massages.

33. Overexertion: Sports and Exercise Injury

All that exercise that's so good for you can also bring pain and toxic side effects. If you've been injured, read section 29 in chapter VI, Illness, Injury, and Healing, for specific preventive and antidote treatments.

Prevention

Common sense tells you how to prevent overexertion and injuries, but what about the sore muscles that can come with even a modest workout, short walk, or careful game? Warming up and stretching your muscles will give you some protection before engaging in any kind of exercise. Consult with trainers or manuals to learn the proper warm-ups and stretches for your activity.

Antidotes

To sooth sore muscles, which are actually caused by the release of lactic acid, and to help eliminate toxins that are released by exercise (which is a good thing, because the whole point of exercise is to strengthen your systems, provide a physical release for emotions and stress—and release stored toxins), try the following:

BROWN RICE VINEGAR BATH: This helps eliminate toxins and waste products, and prevents/treats sore muscles by neutralizing lactic acid, which makes muscles sore. The bath soothes your muscles and stimulates circulation as well. It's good for all skin types and you can indulge as often as needed. Wash in the shower first, then relax for 15 to 20 minutes in a bath to which you've added two cups of brown rice vinegar. Rinse lightly and dry off.

RICE WINE BATH: This will stimulate your circulation, soothe your muscles, and detox. Wash in the shower, first, then fill the bath with hot water and add two quarts of rice wine (sake). Soak for 30 minutes. Don't be surprised if the bathwater is dirty after your half hour—that's just proof of how well the sake detoxes you through your skin. Rinse. This bath is okay for all skin types, but should only be used once per week.

HOT SPRINGS BATH: Make your own hot springs at home by adding three tablespoons of baking soda to your bathwater (you should wash in the shower first). Soak for 15 minutes, but don't rinse. This at-home treat detoxes, soothes muscles, relieves aches and pains, stimulates circulation, relaxes you, and softens your skin. It's good for all skin types, so use it as often as you'd like.

AROMATHERAPY BATH: Wash first in the shower, then draw a bath. Add three drops of marjoram and two drops of lemon essential oil to the bath. Soak for 15 minutes. This will help detox and sooth muscles.

AROMATHERAPY MASSAGE/BODY RUB: To one tablespoon of a natural cream base or vegetable oil, add 5 drops of eucalyptus oil, 5 drops of peppermint oil, and 5 drops of ginger. Use for massage or body rub, particularly on overworked areas, as it soothes and detoxes.

Remember to drink at least eight glasses of pure water each day, and plenty more while you are exercising. To avoid dehydration and electrolyte imbalance, have a sports drink before, during, and after exercise. Gatorade and others replenish vital electrolytes while they rehydrate. This is especially important if you're exercising or playing a game in the heat for more than just a couple of minutes.

34. High-Risk Outdoor Activities

Thrill seekers and adventurers beware: All that skydiving, mountain climbing, car racing, bungee jumping, hang-gliding, white-water rafting, hiking, stunt flying, and weekend warrior stuff become toxic situations when you are injured, suffer from overexertion, or from overexposure to sun and the elements, or come in contact with toxins in food or the environment. You'll find chapters in this book that deal with each of these toxic situations. See chapter VI, Illness, Injury, and Healing; chapter V, Food; and chapter III, Environment. Also see section 36, *In The Spotlight:* The Great Outdoors, in this chapter.

Many high-risk outdoor activities are methods we use to express emotions and deal with stress. To learn more about stress, see chapter II, Emotional and Spiritual Stress.

High-risk activities can also cause plenty of physical stress, strain, and injury. See section 33, Overexertion: Sports and Exercise Injury, in this chapter. Repeated physical strain to the body can lead to degenerative diseases and chronic disorders. The most high-profile examples are professional athletes who, as a result of repeated injuries, end up with an array of permanent problems, ranging from destroyed cartilage to arthritis.

35. Toxins in Creative Arts and Hobbies

Any time you come in contact with chemicals in any creative arts or hobbies, you are at risk for toxic side effects. You'll find more information about specific toxins and chemicals in chapter III, Environment.

Prevention

Whenever possible, use nontoxic products, which can be found in specialty stores and through catalogs (see Resources at the end of the book). Make sure you have adequate ventilation in your work-space in order to disperse fumes from toxic products. Open doors and windows, and follow all safety precautions on product labels. For extra measure, wear a mask (available at pharmacies and health products stores) to reduce exposure to fumes and particles. Protect your hands with gloves, particularly if you use toxic products on a prolonged or regular basis, and wear goggles or special glasses to protect your eyes.

Antidotes

In the case of ingestion, or skin or eye contact, follow guidelines on product labels, including directions regarding circumstances when it's necessary to call poison control or paramedics.

To help your body detox from even mild exposure to chemicals (from your oil painting hobby, for example), follow the All-Purpose Antidotes at the beginning of Part Three. In particular, on days of exposure you'll want to use the skin and hair detoxing antidotes, drink at least eight glasses of pure water each day, take dandelion root, and help your body flush out toxins quickly with bodywork, particularly lymphatic drainage massage and relaxing detox baths (see recipes for Brown Rice Vinegar Bath, Rice Wine Bath, and Hot Springs Bath in the All-Purpose Antidotes and again in the Overexertion: Sports & Exercise Injury section).

In the Spotlight

36. The Great Outdoors

Ah, the toxic possibilities of the Great Outdoors! It's a wonderful place, but it does have its risks. In case you happen to be frolicking near a toxic site of any kind, you'll want to read chapter III, Environment, for prevention and antidote information. For less dramatic encounters, here are a few prevention and antidote tips:

BEE STINGS: Make a paste of Adolph's natural meat tenderizer (available in supermarkets) and water. Rub gently on the bite. The same active ingredient—papaya enzyme—in the tenderizer that breaks down the toughness in meat will draw out the toxins of a bee bite. Ice will help numb the pain of a sting and reduce swelling.

INSECT REPELLENT: Insects, including mosquitos and ants, will stay away when you use peppermint essential oil on cotton balls or insect strips which you can make yourself out of ribbon or paper. Place around your tent, campsite, cabin, campfire, sleeping bag, bed, anywhere you need to be protected (this also works at home). Do not apply the oils directly to your skin, as they can be irritating. Lavender and red thyme essential oils are also good mosquito repellents on cotton balls, insect strips, and your clothing. Place one drop of essential oil on the the bottom of your pants leg, the top of your socks, or anywhere else on clothing. Use only pure essential oils, since they will not stain and have active ingredients.

OTHER BITES: If you're on the beach and have been bitten by a jellyfish or other sea or sand creature, quickly see the lifeguard for first aid. If there is no lifeguard, the Adolph's natural meat tenderizer antidote (see bee sting above) will help draw out toxins; ice will help reduce pain and swelling, and aloe gel will help start healing. But if you have been bitten by something you can't identify, or if the site of the bite is very uncomfortable, begins to swell a lot, involves broken skin or a puncture, or you develop any other symptoms (dizziness, fever or hot flash, clamminess, nausea, breathing difficulty, extreme itching), get to a hospital or call the paramedics immediately. The same advice applies to any other environment you find yourself in when bitten. In the case of snakebites, do not poke at or move the part that has been bitten, since doing so will only spread the venom. Gently wash off the bite (without pressing on it or moving it) to rinse away any venom that may be on the surface. Apply a drop of lavender essential oil to the bite as often as needed; and tie something around your leg or arm near the site of the bite in order to slow down circulation and dispersion of the toxins. Get medical help immediately!

SUNBURN AND WINDBURN: Aloe is your skin's best friend—it heals sunburn and windburn, as well as cuts and scratches, quickly, and it is also soothing. Use only 100 percent pure aloe gel, either directly from the inside of the aloe plant's leaves or from handy plastic bottles you can buy at health stores. The bottled aloe must be 100 percent and its other ingredients must be only in the form of natural preservatives—usually some form of citrus extract and vitamins C, A, and E. Once opened, the bottled aloe must be refrigerated or kept in a cooler. To treat sunburn and windburn, apply the gel (it has a very liquid consistency) to all affected areas and let dry a few minutes before putting on clothing. Reapply as often as you like. Aloe can also protect your lips and other sensitive areas from the elements. Apply as often as you'd like, but don't lick your lips for a few minutes. Wait for the aloe to dry.

SCRATCHES, SCRAPES: After applying an antiseptic, apply 100 percent aloe gel (see directions under sunburn). Cover with a Band-Aid, bandage or gauze. Reapply and redress at least twice a day.

COLD EXPOSURE: Remove all wet clothing from the area, warm skin with either warm (not hot!) water or layers of clothing, blankets, or fabric made of natural fibers. Seek medical attention to reduce risk of effects of hypothermia or frostbite.

SWIMMING POOL: Many swimming pools are disinfected with chlorine, a toxic gas that can cause irritation to eyes, hair, skin, and mucous membranes. Stay out of a freshly chlorinated pool (you won't be allowed into a public pool right after it's been chlorinated; follow safety directions if you have a pool at home), because the gas can irritate your throat, lungs, and respiratory tract.

Bromine is also used to disinfect pools because its effects are less irritating than chlorine's. For your home pool, your best disinfecting choice is an ozone generator—ozone has no toxic effects.

INJURIES: See section 29 on Injury, in chapter VI, and see section 33, Overexertion, in this chapter.

SALTWATER: Saltwater can irritate your skin, especially if you have any cuts, scratches, or freshly shaved areas. Wash off the irritated area with fresh, unsalted water, then apply 100 percent aloe gel (see directions under sunburn above) as often as you'd like.

DRINKING WATER: When you're out in nature, only drink pure bottled water, which you should carry with you. If you ingest tainted water, seek medical attention immediately.

FOOD: All perishable foods must be refrigerated or kept in a cooler with plenty of ice. When perishable food is unrefrigerated, bacteria begin to grow immediately, and after two hours enough has grown to give you a whopping case of food poisoning. To be safe, get food back into the fridge or cooler within a half hour after eating. If the meal lasts more than a half hour, keep hot foods hot—at over 140 degrees—and put cold foods back in the fridge or cooler. If you are out in the sun or in heat over 80 degrees, do this within ten minutes. Don't make the mistake of thinking that just because it's cooked it's okay to leave it out—it is *not* okay.

If you become ill after eating outdoors, watermelon will neutralize stomach acid, and ginger tea or capsules will calm nausea. Seek immediate medical attention if you suspect food poisoning.

IF YOU ARE ON MEDICATIONS: Make sure you ask your holistic physician or health care practitioners what effect, if any, your outdoor activities will have on you.

PHYSICAL ACTIVITY: You can easily become dehydrated when you are physically active in any weather, and extra precautions must be taken for heat and sun. See section 33, Overexertion: Sports and Exercise Injury, earlier in this chapter for information on water intake.

SUNSCREEN: Use only a natural nontoxic sunscreen, available at any health food store. We do not know the long-term effects of chemical sunscreens, and oddly, skin cancer rates have actually increased since the widespread use of sunscreens. Natural, nontoxic sunscreens are formulated with herbs, botanicals, and nutrients that are also free of side effects or any toxic risk, and include ingredients such as octymethoxycinnamate (a natural cinnamon derivative), wild pansy, and coffee extract.

CONTACT WITH ANIMALS: Do not try to make friends with the grizzly bears. Do not touch the wildlife—they may be carrying rabies. If you are bitten by an animal, seek medical attention immediately. The animal may have rabies. Rabies is fatal, but rabies shots will keep you from developing the disease. You must have a rabies shot after being bitten and *before* rabies symptoms begin or you will die if the animal that bit you had rabies.

The Male Body, Mind, and Spirit

37. The Reproductive System

As you'll recall from the description of how the male reproductive system works in the section on the reproductive system in Part One, the testes (or testicles) are glands that produce the male sex hormone testosterone and sperm, the male reproductive cells that will ultimately travel out of the body to fertilize the female egg. Testosterone and the other male hormones produced in other glands of the body control the male secondary sex characteristics, which begin to appear at puberty—the growth of the penis, growth of body hair, deepening of the voice, and larger muscle mass.

Sperm travel from the testes through a number of ducts, then mixes with fluid from the seminal vesicles, a thick whitish fluid secreted by the prostate gland, and fluid from the urethra. Altogether, this makes up the sperm-carrying liquid called semen, which is expelled from the body by the penis.

Prevention

To prevent problems associated with hormone imbalance, malfunction, disorder or disease of the male reproductive system and the toxic effects that result, reduce your exposure to all toxins, both external and those created internally. Follow a balanced, low-fat natural diet, drink at least eight glasses of pure water each day to help flush out your body's wastes and toxins efficiently and consistently, and use the All-Purpose Antidotes as preventive measures. Treat each and every condition that arises in as natural and as nontoxic a way as possible, with the help of a naturopathic physician or other holistic health care professional. Fertility difficulties and impotence often have physical roots in toxic complications, and impotence often has an emotional/psychological cause that can be remedied through counseling, meditative, stress-reduction techniques. (Prostate problems, including cancer, are addressed separately in the following section.)

Lymphatic drainage massage can be a valuable preventive measure to promote the elimination of toxins, particularly for the reproductive system, since it lies near the lymph glands on either side of the groin area.

Antidotes

Use the All-Purpose Antidotes, cut back or cut out your consumption of alcohol (it can contribute to impotence), have lymphatic drainage massage on a regular basis by a professional, and massage all of your lymph glands in the shower with soap, or afterward with body lotion, for a few minutes every day. The glands are located just below the ears and jaw on either side of your neck; on the left and right sides of the middle of your chest, just below your collarbone; at the bottom of and under each armpit; and on either side of the groin, where your thigh meets your torso. This last location, since it is so near the reproductive organs, should get the most attention in order to clear toxins, relieve clogging, and help disperse lymph fluid.

To help increase fertility, avoid tight, restrictive clothing in the groin area.

38. Prostate Problems

The prostate gland is actually a cluster of glands the size of a walnut that surrounds the urethra, the tube that carries urine from the bladder and semen as it leaves the body. The prostate secretes the thick, whitish fluid that comprises most of semen, the fluid that transports sperm.

As men age (usually after age forty), the prostate can become inflamed, a condition known as prostatitis. When this happens, because the gland surrounds the urethra, the swollen prostate interferes with the passage of urine. The same happens in the case of prostate enlargement, known as benign prostatic hyperplasia (BPH). In both cases, as well as with prostate cancer, testosterone is the culprit, binding to the prostate and causing not only enlargement and inflammation, but cancer as well.

An enlarged or cancerous prostate results when testosterone converts to dihydrotestosterone (DHT), and DHT then binds to receptor sites on the membranes of prostate cells and their nuclei. Too much DHT can cause the prostate's cells to divide and multiply at an abnormally high rate, leading to enlargement, cancer or, both. More often than not, prostate cancer is silent, showing few or no symptoms until it has progressed.

The mainstream medicine way of dealing with prostate problems or prostate cancer has been surgery to remove prostate tissue, or the entire prostate, and radiation. Both operations can not only leave the patient with temporary and permanent problems of incontinence, sexual dysfunction and impotence, and scarring of the urinary passage (which can lead to more blockage), but they do not address the *cause* of the problem, and so recurrence is common.

Mainstream medicine gives men drugs that sharply reduce their levels of testosterone. This results in a real hormonal nightmare. The lack of testosterone causes sexual dysfunction, impotency, and impairment, and other system-wide conditions.

There is no need to get rid of the testosterone. There is only a need to keep it from converting into dihydrotestosterone (DHT) and to keep DHT from binding to the prostate's receptor sites. That, fortunately, can be accomplished so easily, painlessly, and without any side effects you won't believe it.

Prevention and Antidotes

There is an herb called saw palmetto *(Serenosa repens),* and if you take a 160 mg. saw palmetto pill twice each day, you can prevent prostate enlargement, inflammation, and prostate cancer. If you already have prostate cancer, saw palmetto stands an excellent chance of curing you. If your cancer has spread to other areas of your body, that will complicate matters and necessitate different treatments, but saw palmetto will stop the production of cancer cells in the prostate itself and will restore prostate function.

How does the herb work? Simply, saw palmetto prevents the conversion of testosterone to dihydrotestosterone (DHT), and also keeps DHT from binding to the receptor sites of the prostate cells. Without the interference of DHT, your prostate cells will not multiply at an abnormally high rate.

Medical studies have proven saw palmetto's effectiveness and clinical tests on patients proves the same. The PSA blood test that screens for the presence of prostate cancer shows that the use of saw palmetto brings the "PSA numbers" back into the normal range.

The saw palmetto berry extract is nontoxic; you can stay on it indefinitely. Beginning in their late thirties men should take it daily to prevent prostate problems. The extract you take should be concentrated and purified, and contain 85 to 90 percent fatty acids and sterols. This information will appear on the label.

Although mainstream physicians are slowly catching on to the value of saw palmetto, their patients, and men in general, are way ahead of them. The demand for the herb has increased so dramatically in recent years that farmers, pickers, and packers report a tremendous increase in production to keep up. Saw palmetto is native to the southeastern United States. Prices are reasonable; around $14.98 for a bottle of one hundred capsules, which, when you take two capsules a day as a preventive or for treatment, will provide you with almost a two-month supply.

Consult with a naturopathic or holistic physician if you suspect prostate problems, or if you are already being treated for them, and request saw palmetto as your treatment. Ayurvedic-trained and Chinese Medicine–trained physicians will also be supportive of this natural treatment. Mainstream doctors will be reluctant to let go of surgical, chemotherapy, and radiation treatments, because they generate millions and millions of dollars every year (prostate problems are extremely common in men over fifty) for specialists, surgeons, hospitals, and the pharmaceutical industry. But, as more patients demand the noninvasive, nontoxic saw palmetto as treatment, and say no thank you to the debilitating mainstream alternatives that do not address the cause of prostate problems and prostate cancer, the mainstream medical community will eventually turn around, as they have done with other treatments. Saw palmetto research and study in Europe and in the United States is one of the fastest growing research areas, with excellent results. Many enlightened mainstream physicians have already incorporated saw palmetto into their prevention treatment plans for their patients, and in time it will be the main method of treatment (especially when all those male urologists find that it is saving their own prostates and their own lives).

In the Spotlight

39. The High Risk of Being Male

*I*n his recent book, *The Male Mystique,* Andrew Kimbrell noted the following chilling realities:

- Men have more illnesses than women.
- Men live 10 percent fewer years than women.
- Men constitute 75 percent of all alcoholics.
- Men commit suicide at four times the rate of women.
- Men are stressed by society's economic expectations and are discouraged from being vulnerable and creative.
- Men most often lose their children in custody cases.
- Men have been turned into "money machines" and "success objects," overcompetitive humans who view their entire bodies, minds, and beings as machines.
- Men are conditioned to seek external power.
- Men, in far, far, greater numbers than women get killed and maimed in war.
- Men are uncomfortable with these images and are desperately searching for their true identities.

- The current male identity is closely tied to job and money.
- Some of these same problems are now affecting working women; and we see it manifesting in, among other things, their health, stress levels, and increasing addictions.

Society hardly prepares a man to live an emotionally and spiritually fully balanced life, and because of this his physical health suffers as well as every aspect of his life.

Men, then, are at greater risk for the toxic effects discussed in this book. Studies have shown, time and again, that when men suppress their emotions and act in the way that society pressures them to act, they are at exceedingly high risk for every malady imaginable, from ulcers to heart attacks, from high blood pressure to cancer, from abusive acting out to mass murder, from anxiety to depression, from listlessness to acute unfulfillment.

Studies also show that men's scores in psychological tests to measure emotional issues are the exact opposite from women's scores: very high on the need for external power, and very low on the desire for human connections. These findings correspond to companion studies showing that people who value relationships more than external power have stronger hearts and immune systems and suffer from fewer illnesses. Men, then, are more often plagued by heart problems, weak immune systems, and illness. The correlation between stress and power-seeking behavior emerges as another link that shows harm to the male immune system more often than to the female immune system.

The prevention and treatment of all the risks associated with being a man lie in how a man views himself and how society views him and pressures him to view himself. In the past thirty years, we have shown improvement in this area (coincidentally, as women have become at higher risk for traditionally male hazards), so perhaps now more than ever before men are being actively encouraged to break out of this restrictive mold.

The first step in detoxing from this unhealthy behavior is to recognize that it exists. Then, take active steps to replace the old, limiting, unhealthy ideals of what it is to be a man with new, healthier ones. From these new attitudes will spring better physical health as well. Men should pay particular attention to the recommendations in chapter II, Emotional and Spiritual Stress, for these reasons.

And, to provide for the evolution of better health for men, we can all focus on educating boys about their full human potential from the time they are born.

❧ IX ❧

Travel

40. Domestic and Foreign Travel

*I*t's supposed to be fun, and it does broaden your horizons, but often travel can be stressful and toxic—the planning, the packing, the downside of whatever methods of transportation you choose, different food, different water, different environment, increased risk of catching some bug, and trying to cram too much into each day. We always swear we're somehow going to make it less of an ordeal next time. Perhaps with some of these tips you can.

You'll find information specific to flying in section 42, *In the Spotlight:* Air Travel and Jet Lag.

Prevention and Antidotes

Two days before you leave on your trip, begin strengthening your immune system by taking echinacea liquid (*angustifolia* species only) (see section 31, *In The Spotlight:* Cold and Flu in chapter VI, Illness, Injury, and Healing, for more on echinacea). Use this preventive dosage: Take one dropperful if you are 150 pounds or over, one-half dropperful if you are under 150 pounds, and stir in a cup of pure water, juice, or tea. Drink once in the morning and once at night on the two days before you leave. Continue the dosage while you are away, but if the two prior days and the length of the trip total more than two weeks, stop the echinacea after the fourteenth day. Resume after five days, if you become sick during or after your trip.

DOMESTIC TRAVEL. Drink only pure bottled water, since a change in local water systems may upset your stomach. Continue with some form of exercise during your trip, even if it's just walking or doing stretches when you get up in the morning and before bed. Ginger tea, ginger capsules, and special wristbands that press on an acupressure point will prevent and relieve nausea from car or other ground travel, seasickness, air sickness, altitude sickness, or other causes. When traveling to higher altitudes than you are accustomed to, take precautions to prevent altitude sickness: drink plenty of pure water and eat plenty of fruit for a few days before and on the day of your trip; eat frequent, small meals to keep your blood sugar even; and take occasional deep breaths to adjust to the lower amount of oxygen at high altitudes (but don't hyperventilate). You may experience dizziness, light-headedness, sleepiness, and mild nausea on your first day or two at higher altitudes, but if you have other symptoms, seek medical attention right away. Avoid overexertion, too, during the first day or two at high altitude to help prevent altitude sickness.

In hotel rooms, to lower your risk of catching the bug of the person who last had your room or any other organic toxin, bring along a few bottles of antibacterial, antiviral, antifungal, antiseptic disinfectant essential oils, which are thyme, lavender, and eucalyptus radiata (not plain eucalyptus). These come in small bottles, tinier than lipstick, so are easy to carry. Wipe the mattress, toilet seat, sink faucet handles, doorknobs, telephone handset and mouthpiece with a tissue moistened with a few drops of each of these essential oils. Also bring along a lamp ring to put on one of the lightbulbs, and put a few drops of each of the essential oils in the ring. When you turn on the lamp, the heat will disperse the disinfectant oils into the air and detox it. This may sound like paranoid, compulsive behavior, but many people return home from a trip sick.

FOREIGN TRAVEL. Follow the preventives and antidotes listed above for domestic travel, and add the following: Before leaving on your trip, consult with a physician who specializes in infectious diseases (they're also "travel medicine" specialists) or with one of the many travel medicine centers that are now part of many hospitals. Find out which shots, precautions, and health alerts apply to your particular destination(s), and follow all requirements and recommendations to the letter.

If you are traveling to Canada, you won't have to worry at all about drinking the water or eating any kind of food, unless you are sensitive to local water changes, in which case you'll want to drink only bottled water. For all other countries, consult with your travel medicine physician about food and beverage precautions. Some countries are about as safe for you as the United States; others range from low risk to extremely risky, depending upon the local bacteria (which the locals can tolerate just fine, but will make you very sick), pesticides used in that country, food preparation conditions, and sanitary conditions. As a general rule, when traveling outside the United States and Canada, drink only pure bottled water (preferably a brand like Evian, which comes from one particular, safe source), eat only cooked food, do not put ice in your drinks (ice is created, after all, from the local drinking water), peel all fruit, brush your teeth with bottled water, and don't get water into your mouth while showering. For mild digestive system reactions to the local food and water, use ginger pills and ginger tea as a preventive as well as to treat stomach upset, nausea, and diarrhea. Drink pure water to rehydrate. Anything beyond temporary, mild diarrhea or other reactions should be taken seriously. For diarrhea, stomach pain, nausea, vomiting, fever, chills, or other symptoms, seek medical attention immediately.

IRREGULARITY. Often when we travel, we don't move our bowels with the same frequency as we do back home. For more on this see the next section, Recovering from Your Trip, and apply the preventive measures and antidotes for the duration of your trip, as well as when you return.

41. Recovering from Your Trip

How often have we heard, or said ourselves, "I need a vacation from my vacation!"? This can be especially true of intense business trips, too, when we have had no leisure time at all. When traveling for fun, we tend to do too much, to cram in as much as we can. When we get home, the recuperation begins.

Prevention

Try not to wear yourself out on your vacation, and do whatever you can to minimize your exposure to toxins while you're traveling. Unfortunately, it's a common occurrence for people to become "irregular" when they travel. You do not move your bowels with the same frequency as you do at home, so you may be storing more toxins in your body during your trip. To prevent illness when you return home, practice as many detoxifying preventive measures and antidotes as you can while you're traveling. Don't leave your healthy routine behind just because you're out of town. When you return, you should boost your immune system to prevent the all too common cold, flu, lethargy, and other conditions we're prone to after traveling, not only from exhaustion, but from bugs we may have picked up, and from the toxic reactions to a different environment, different food, and crazy schedule. Take one dropperful of echinacea (*angustifolia* species only) liquid if you are 150 pounds or more, or one-half dropperful if you weigh less than 150 pounds, twice a day in a cup of juice, water, or tea, for two days.

Use any of the All-Purpose Antidotes as preventive measures, too.

Antidotes

Use the All-Purpose Antidotes to get your systems back on track. You may want to schedule bodywork, massage, or lymphatic drainage massage for shortly after you return home or give yourself an extralong lymphatic drainage massage. To restore your usual bowel movement schedule, do not blast your system with laxative preparations, either pharmaceutical or natural. Go easy, and remember to drink eight glasses of pure water each day. Begin the day with two glasses, to which you've added a teaspoon of lemon juice in each. That will help stimulate a bowel movement. So will dried fruits like prunes and raisins, or a bowl of good old-fashioned raisin bran cereal. You do

not need to go into a high-fiber frenzy. That will only shock and irritate your systems. Often, a few sips of coffee will be enough to send
you to the bathroom. If you weren't able to restore your usual routine while you were on your trip, make sure you do it on your first
day back, or the morning of the next day. Often just being home will
stimulate the mind-body connection and you'll be back on track
within hours. Bodywork and massage will also help stimulate your
elimination system.

In the Spotlight

42. Air Travel and Jet Lag

*A*irplanes present their own unique environment, and jet lag is their
own unique malady.

In a plane you are faced with extremely dry air; a cabin pressurized to the equivalent of the altitude of a city at 5,000 feet (like
Denver); recycled air that also recycles everyone's exhaled, coughed,
and sneezed germs; motion that can cause you to become dizzy,
queasy, or nauseous; food that can, on occasion, give you indigestion or make you sick; narrow seats with little legroom, which can
create circulation problems in your legs if you fly often enough or
long enough; and required pesticide spraying of the passenger cabin
before disembarking in some countries.

If you've flown between time zones you are prone to jet lag,
and the more time zones you go through, the worse it will be.
That's because your internal body clock will be out of sync with society once you land. Back home it may be 11:00 P.M., so your body
clock says it's time to go to sleep. But, where you've just landed, it
is 6:00 A.M. and the locals are just getting up. When you arrive, it
won't be evening, it will be the morning of the next day. So, do you
go right to sleep or do you try to adapt immediately to the new time,
have breakfast, and go through the day having missed an entire
night's sleep?

Jet lag also causes problems with your other systems. You may experience indigestion, constipation, fatigue, insomnia, headaches, and other symptoms that reflect abrupt and radical changes in sleep, activity, and eating times and patterns.

You can begin your prevention of the toxic effects of flying and jet lag before you ever leave the ground—or your house, for that matter.

Air Travel

The day before you fly, begin to boost your immune system by taking the preventive dosages of echinacea (see section 40, Domestic and Foreign Travel) and 1,000 mg. of Ester C (vitamin C) in the morning and at night, and continue for the length of your trip. Drink glasses of pure water in flight, and avoid alcohol and caffeine since they are diuretics, and the dry air in the plane's cabin is already dehydrating. Also, alcohol has a greater effect on you in the pressurized cabin than it does on the ground. To counteract the dry air in the cabin (with dry nasal passages, mouth, and throat, you're more susceptible to picking up a cold, flu, or other illness), wet a handkerchief with pure water and hold it to your nose periodically during the flight in order to breathe more moist air.

Stretch your legs and walk around at least once every hour during the flight. With your legs in such cramped quarters, your circulation becomes impaired (and if you already have circulation problems, this puts you at especially high risk); the blood in your legs can clot, and a clot can easily travel to your lungs. If you are on a long flight or travel frequently, this is especially important.

If your destination is out of the country, you may be on a flight on which the cabin is sprayed with pesticides before passengers disembark. The country that requires spraying may not be your final destination, just a stop before the plane takes off again, but check the list below to see if there is one on your route. Most countries don't require airlines to spray when the passengers are still onboard, but, unfortunately, as of this writing the following still do:

Argentina	Kenya
Barbados	Madagascar
Congo	Mauritius
Grenada	Mozambique
India	Trinidad/Tobago

These pesticides are toxic and can cause allergic reactions, respiratory distress, and flu-like symptoms. Repeated exposure has been known to cause multiple chemical sensitivity disorder.

If you are pregnant, asthmatic, or allergic to pesticides, ask your doctor to write a note exempting you from remaining onboard during spraying. (Come to think of it, even if you are healthy as a horse, ask your doctor for a note!) Show the note to the flight attendant when you first board the plane. Prior to landing, remind the flight attendant of your exemption. If you don't have a note and must remain onboard during spraying, cover yourself with an airline blanket (not your own blanket or clothing, as it will get contaminated by the toxic pesticide) before the spraying begins. When spraying is completed, wait a few moments for the spray to settle to the ground before removing the blanket. You may also want to cover your nose and mouth with a health mask, which you can buy in any pharmacy or health food store.

Jet Lag

To help prevent the effects of jet lag, for a few days before and after the flight take the herb ginseng in tablet, liquid, or tea form, three times per day, and a 25 mg. vitamin B-complex capsule once in the morning and once at night with food.

Set your watch to the current time of your destination as soon as you board the plane. If you arrive during the day, get as much sunshine as you can. Even though you may be tired, do not go to sleep until it's evening at your destination. This will help you adapt quickly and will greatly reduce the effects of jet lag. It will make you feel as if you stayed up a very long time before going to bed, rather than totally confusing your inner time clock.

Before bed, a relaxing warm shower will help soothe the stress of your first day in the new time zone. Then, sleep as long as you like. You may feel a bit more tired than usual on your second day, but by the end of the day you will have begun to adjust. Eat lightly, but frequently, during the first and second days in order to keep your blood sugar levels even. Drink plenty of pure bottled water and try not to schedule anything strenuous. To work the kinks out of your body after your flight, try gentle stretching or yoga exercises and a massage by a professional (many hotels have health clubs), your traveling partner, or give yourself a gentle massage.

❧ X ❧

Times of Life

43. Infancy

It's a boy! It's a girl! It's living in my house, now what do I do?

Your naturopathic or holistic pediatrician will guide you through the maze of caring for your baby, but you should remember that babies and children are far more sensitive to all toxic activity than adults are.

On your baby's first day outside the womb, detoxification decisions are already being made. Just a few hours after babies are born they are given an injection of vitamin K to reduce the risk of death from bleeding. However, studies show that those babies who are given vitamin K by injection are two times more likely to get childhood cancer than babies who are given their vitamin K orally.

You must ask for oral vitamin K for your baby, because doctors routinely give it by injection. Researchers believe that the injection is a problem because phenol, a carcinogenic substance, is used in the preparation of the vitamin K concoction. The newborn can detoxify the phenol receiving it orally, but not when it's going directly into the baby's bloodstream by injection. When given by injection, Vitamin K requires only one dose. When given orally, it requires repeated doses.

Another toxic tidbit you may not be aware of: Honey is extremely toxic to children under the age of two. Never give it to them.

44. Childhood

Because babies and children are far more sensitive to all toxic activity, it is extremely important that they be raised in as toxin-free environment as possible (see chapter III, Environment). Their systems cannot tolerate the levels of lead, for example, often found in tap water (and is still in lead paint), levels that, while they certainly aren't good for adults, do not do nearly as much damage to adults as the children.

Your children will also have a much stronger reaction to the chemicals and natural toxins in food (see chapter V, Food) and should cut out as much processed food as possible and eat only organic produce.

Children are far more sensitive to medications and are always prescribed smaller doses than adults. Part of this has to do with the sensitivity of their growing bodies, and part with their lower weight. Some adults, however, would be wise to stick to medication doses in certain circumstances that are closer to children's doses when they weigh under 101 pounds or have systems that they know are particularly sensitive to certain medications.

The same goes for any natural medications you may want to give your children: They cannot take the same dosages that you can. Typically, a child's dose is half that of an adult's, but it may be even lower in certain circumstances. Always check with your naturopathic or holistic pediatrician or other natural health care practitioner before giving your children any natural medicines, including herbs, nutritional supplements, and the like.

45. Adolescence

Junk food, poor diet, hormonal changes, rebellion, growth spurts, acne—adolescence can be a toxic time of life.

Children and adolescents can use the All-Purpose Antidotes listed at the beginning of Part Three and the other antidotes throughout this book as long as dosages are reduced to compensate for their age and weight. Check with your naturopathic pediatrician or holistic physician to determine proper dosages for your child and his or her particular sensitivities.

Plenty of pure water and natural foods are a must in the teen years, when the temptation to live on pizza and soda will override even the most health-conscious teen's better judgment. The water, good diet, and daily exercise will help an adolescent's systems to detoxify naturally. Bodywork, massage, and lymphatic drainage massage are also highly recommended, as they are perfectly safe at any age.

Emotions run rampant during adolescent years as hormones kick in and he or she must deal with all the common teen stresses (see chapter II, Emotional and Spiritual Stress). Now would be a good time to explain the importance of stress-reduction techniques, meditative experiences, and release of emotions.

46. Adulthood

Congratulations, you're legal! This means that you are now permitted by the U.S. government to indulge in the toxic activities of smoking and drinking.

If you're going to do that, see chapter I, Addictions and Habits, for how to detox from the adult privileges you had to sneak around to indulge in before.

During specific phases of adulthood, your body, mind, and spirit will be faced with particular toxic stresses they may not have had to deal with before. As you read on, in the sections Parenthood, Midlife, and Sixty-Plus, you'll learn about those phases. But for the phase between the ages of eighteen and when you become a parent (or up to about thirty-five, if you're not a parent), you face the usual toxic risks—the ones that are presented in all fifty entries of Part Three.

Adulthood will, of course, take some getting used to, and if you're new to it, you'll want to get a jump on those who have already been in it for awhile and form some healthy toxin-free habits from the start.

47. Parenthood

No matter how old you are when you become a parent, you're going to be faced with a whole new world of toxic possibilities.

If you're a woman, see chapter IV, The Female Body, Mind, and Spirit, for information on pregnancy, childbirth, and the postnatal period, as well as chapter II, Emotional and Spiritual Stress. That chapter will tell you how to cope with all the aspects of stress, which will no doubt be increased by motherhood.

If you're a man, see chapter VIII, The Male Body, Mind, and Spirit, in particular section 39, *In the Spotlight:* The High Risk of Being Male. Also see chapter II, Emotional and Spiritual Stress, for obvious reasons.

You're going to be tired, you're going to be frustrated, you're going to wonder if you're doing the right things. This is normal. You're going to be so busy taking care of your children that you will neglect your own physical, emotional, and spiritual health. Don't do that. If you are even remotely tempted to play martyr, remember that it's also in the best interests of your children for you to be physically, emotionally, and spiritually healthy. So if you're not going to do it for yourself, then at least do it for your kids.

Somehow you will survive parenthood, and if you take good care of yourself, the process will be much healthier and stress-free. Don't shy away from asking for all kinds of help and information from health care practitioners, compassionate and empowering friends and family, and support groups when dealing with children and parenthood issues. Educate yourself even further with books, tapes, videos, lectures, and the incredible wealth of information available via computer. Whether you have a spouse, significant other, or you are a single parent, there is plenty of support for you, just for the asking.

48. Midlife

If you're lucky, you'll have your traditional midlife crisis early; in your late twenties, say, before you've gotten too entrenched and have too much to have a crisis over.

But if you're like most people, you'll do your "midlife reevaluation" (a kinder word for crisis) somewhere between thirty-five and forty-five. This is a time, not so ironically, when a lifetime of less than ideal health choices will begin to catch up with you, so while you're reevaluating the Meaning of Life and where your life fits into that, you'll also begin to feel many of the physical, emotional, and spiritual consequences of a life that needs some detoxing.

Midlife is a time of immense personal and professional change. To cope with all of that, pay particular attention to chapter I, Addictions and Habits; chapter II, Emotional and Spiritual Stress (you may more than once find yourself reading section 12, *In The Spotlight*: Toxic People, Toxic Choices), and chapter VIII, The Male Body, Mind, and Spirit, section 39, *In the Spotlight*: The High Risk of Being Male. If you are experiencing any health difficulties, other sections of this book will take on even more urgent meaning for you.

Midlife is the ideal time to step up your healthy, detoxifying way of life, or initiate one if you haven't been particularly health-conscious previously. You see, as we approach forty, we begin to realize that we are approximately midway through our lifespan, that probably fewer years lie before us than are already behind us, and if we're not careful, we won't always feel as good as we do now. In fact, we may begin to feel some of the effects of toxicity and less-than-diligent care of our health. Up to this point we all figure there's plenty of time ahead of us. We feel so immortal in our youth that if we go awhile without exercise, or we overdo alcohol, cigarettes, junk food, and the other no-no's, . . . well, we think it won't really matter that much. Besides, we don't feel a lot of the bad effects of our behavior during our first thirty or so years (unless we've really gone hog-wild on the no-no's). But then, all of a sudden—at the forty-mark—it can all begin to catch up with us.

This is pretty much your last chance to undo the damage you've done before it has the opportunity to get really serious.

Go for it—you'll feel better.

Oh, and by the way, remember the old saying—"Life begins at forty."

Here are a few quotes to help you through the bumpy parts:

Life is ours to be spent, not to be saved.
—D. H. Lawrence

The fishermen know that the sea is dangerous and the storm terrible, but they have never found these dangers sufficient reason for remaining ashore.
—Vincent Van Gogh

If you don't get everything you want, think of the things you don't get that you don't want.
—Oscar Wilde

What lies behind us and what lies before us are tiny matters compared with what lies within us.
—Anonymous

Never put off until tomorrow what you can do today, because if you enjoy it today, you can do it again tomorrow.
—Anonymous

Even if you're on the right track, you'll get run over if you just sit there.
—Will Rogers

Confusion is a word we have invented for an order which is not understood.
—Henry Miller

When all else is lost, the future still remains.
—Christian Nestell Bovee

The absurd man is the one who never changes.
—Auguste M. Barthelemy

If we insist on being as sure as is conceivable, in every step of our course, we must be content to creep along the ground, and can never soar.
—John Henry Newman

Begin to weave, and God will give you the thread.
—German proverb

Remember what you have seen, because everything forgotten returns to the circling winds.
—Navajo wind chant

He who obtains has little; He who scatters has much.
—Lao-Tse

A man's soul will teach him. There is no man who is not incessantly taught by his soul.
—Rabbi Pinhas

49. Sixty-Plus

You're older, wiser, and your body has very different needs than it did in previous decades.

You are more sensitive to toxins than you have ever been since childhood; you need more of some things and less of others.

Here are the highlights:

- Your liver, kidneys, and pancreas function less efficiently, and digestion can become less efficient because of a decrease in the production of stomach acid.
- You absorb vitamin A more efficiently, so it's easier to get a toxic buildup of it. (Don't overdo it on the megavitamin pills!)
- You need more calcium, vitamin B-complex, vitamin D, folic acid, and the antioxidants (vitamin C, E, and beta carotene).
- You are likely to be on more medications, therefore your potential for drug interactions increases.
- You may retain more fluid, in part because of medications.
- You may be constipated more often.

- You are at higher risk for colds and flu developing into pneumonia, so you'll need to incorporate deep breathing and stretching into your daily exercise.

If you've been taking good care of yourself, using natural medicine, and living a low-toxin lifestyle, the years from sixty onward can be as healthy and vibrant as your earlier decades. Consult with your holistic physician and natural health care practitioners when you incorporate more of the natural preventives and antidotes in this book into your life. They will help you address your specific needs and sensitivities. Not every person who is over sixty is the same, as you know. Your health at this point depends upon how you have been taking care of yourself in the past, your attitude about growing older, and how much your health may have been compromised not only by toxic activity but, sad to say, by mainstream medical care.

In the Spotlight

50. Annual Physicals Timeline

*H*as the annual physical gone the way of Dr. Kildare, Ben Casey, and the house call?

Not really. You can still have a complete physical every year, and it may very well be one of the most important prevention steps you can take. But unless you're going in with a specific complaint, your health insurance will probably not cover the cost. Don't be held hostage by your health insurance. An annual physical, including lab costs, will total around $250, a bit less in smaller communities, a bit higher in one of the top five cities. If you can put aside just $10 per week, you can have your annual physical, with as many extras as you'd like to throw in, and have money left over to celebrate your good health afterward with a splendid dinner for two.

Depending on the insurance carrier you have, and whether it's a group or individual policy, an HMO or PPO, the annual physical isn't a frequently covered benefit, so if you want regular exams, look for coverage that provides for them in some way. Most policies, though, are for the diagnosis of a problem. Although this line of health insurance thinking is keeping doctors and patients from preventing illness or catching something early, many states are making progress in this area by making certain types of preventive coverage mandatory, including mammograms and well child care.

Unfortunately, patients are steered away from yearly physicals because of their cost, except for tests like a yearly Pap smear for women or regular treatments for a chronic condition. But physicians would like to see more patients come in for annual physicals, especially those over fifty. Of course, coming in for a physical once a year when you're in your twenties, thirties, and forties is just as important, because that's when you can catch conditions early, like high blood pressure, tumors, cancers, and heart problems. In fact, it's cheaper to do this then, than to wait until you're sick.

Eventually, the health insurance industry will figure that out, too.

You can have your annual physical done by a holistic family practice physician or an internist, and, based on your physical condition and family history, you may also want to have more specific, extensive testing done by a particular specialist.

Some HMOs do provide for an annual physical, but even insurance industry insiders caution that there are some low-quality HMOs out there, resulting in everything from substandard care to incomplete testing, to inaccurate lab results and the unavailability of follow-up care.

With well care for children provided by many insurers, complete annual physicals for kids are routine, but those who participate in school sports will have an initial physical that's more extensive, even before placing foot on a practice field.

Beyond the basic exam, doctors will ask about any weaknesses or conditions that may affect the child's ability to exercise. This also involves looking at risk factors in the child and family for specifics like heart disease, high blood pressure, and sudden death. Still, it is hard to screen for the athlete of any age who suddenly drops dead during practice, a game, or athletic performance, as evidenced by those who've made the news in recent years.

Complete physicals differ for women and men; and children,

teens, and adults of varying ages. They are tailored to your specific needs, based on your individual and family medical history and lifestyle.

The Basic Complete Physical for Adults

1. Physician reviews your complete individual and family medical history, including the condition of your body's systems, your lifestyle and occupational concerns, emotional and stress factors, and medications and/or nutritional supplements you take.
2. Chest X ray.
3. Blood test: includes CBC (blood count), chemistry profile, lipid profile (cholesterol types and levels), thyroid, PSA (prostate screening, for men), HIV (optional, requires written consent).
4. Urinalysis: for kidney and bladder function and screens for specific conditions of all systems.
5. Electrocardiogram (EKG): monitors heart function; noninvasive test that gives an electrical picture of the heart.
6. Blood pressure.
7. Check of reflexes.
8. Monitoring of heart, lungs, abdomen, and arteries in the neck with a stethoscope.
9. Check of throat, ears, eyes.
10. Brief neurological exam.
11. *Men:* prostate exam, breast exam; lesson on how to examine testicles for lumps.
12. *Women:* gynecological exam, pelvic and rectal exam, Pap smear, breast exam, mammogram and sonogram of breasts, sonogram of ovaries for early detection of ovarian cancer.
13. Stress test: Results are only accurate when the test is done on men and women who have a history of heart problems or symptoms of ongoing or new condition.
14. Nutritional and exercise counseling.

Examination Specifics from Childhood Through Adulthood

BIRTH TO FIVE YEARS: Well baby care several times a year includes required and optional vaccinations. Individualized testing is based on child's and family's condition and history. Your pediatrician will schedule vaccinations.

EIGHTEEN MONTHS: First measles vaccination. Second can be any time one year after the first, but should be given before high school; measles outbreaks are common in teens who have not been vaccinated or only partially vaccinated.

TEEN YEARS: Hepatitis B vaccine.

FIFTEEN YEARS: First complete gynecological exam for girls, including Pap smear when they first become sexually active, or by age eighteen.

THIRTY-FIVE YEARS: Baseline mammogram for women who have no family history of breast cancer. With family history, mammogram is done earlier. Your gynecologist will advise based on your individual history and family history. A sonogram can detect cysts and benign and cancerous tumors in women with small or compact breasts that in many cases go undetected by a mammogram. You will probably have to specifically request a sonogram. The sonogram can also supplement an inconclusive mammogram. Also have a sonogram of the pelvic area to check for ovarian cysts, fibroids in the uterus, or abnormal growths in the area.

FORTY YEARS: Mammogram/sonogram every two years for women between forty and fifty with no family history of breast cancer. With family or individual history, your gynecologist will advise on test frequency.

FORTY-FIVE YEARS: *Men:* First PSA prostate blood test to screen for prostate cancer. Earlier if individual or family history warrants. Physician will advise.

FIFTY YEARS: *Women:* Mammogram/sonogram every year after age fifty. *Men and Women:* Colon exam.

Additional Vaccine Information

CHICKEN POX VACCINE: Physician will advise on scheduling for children. Teens and adults who have never had the chicken pox should be vaccinated.

HEPATITIS A VACCINE: Advised if you travel internationally.

DIPHTHERIA-TETANUS (DT) BOOSTER: Every ten years during adulthood. A booster will be given immediately if an injury results in an open wound that may have been contaminated, unless you have received a booster within the six months prior to the injury.

FLU SHOT: Recommended for adults, particularly seniors. Your physician will advise.

PNEUMONIA VACCINE: Protects against bacterial pneumonia, advised for seniors, asthmatics, anyone with lung problems. Your physician will advise.

HEPATITIS B VACCINE: Advised for teens and adults who have never received the vaccination. Particularly important for those who are at risk for contracting Hepatitis B, including health care workers and all who are sexually active.

TRAVEL SHOTS: Vaccinations and other shots based upon the geographical areas you will be visiting. Many hospitals have departments that specialize in travel medicine; infectious disease specialists in private practice can also advise and administer shots.

Resources

Ayurvedic Products

The following companies offer Ayurvedic products via mail order:

Bazaar of India Imports:	(510) 548-4110
Devi, Inc.:	(800) 237-8221
Lotus Herbs:	(408) 479-1667
Maharishi Ayur-Veda:	(800) 255-8332
Tej Beauty Enterprises:	(212) 581-8136
Infinite Possibilities:	(800) 858-1808

Ayurvedic Health Centers

Maharishi Ayur-Veda Health Centers
P.O. Box 282
Fairfield, IA 52556
  (515) 472-8477
Call for a list of Ayurvedic physicians and health centers in your area.

In Canada:
  P.O. Box 6500
  Huntsville, Ontario
  P0A 1K0
  Canada
    (705) 635-2234

Chopra Center for Well-Being
  7590 Fay Avenue, #403
  La Jolla, CA 92037
  (619) 551-7788

Essential Oils and Aromatherapy Products

The following companies provide pure essential oils via mail order:

Simplers Botanical
  Box 39
  Forestville, CA 95436
  (800) 6-JASMIN

3000 BC
  7946 Germantown Avenue
  Philadelphia, PA 19118
  (800) AROMATIC

Aroma Vera
  5901 Rodeo Road
  Los Angeles, CA 90016
  (800) 669-9514

Purple Isle Aromatherapy
  171 Jasmine Street
  Tavernier, FL 33070
  (800) 853-0080; (305) 664-0018

Original Swiss Aromatics
  Pacific Institute of Aromatherapy
  Box 6842
  San Rafael, CA 94903
  (415) 459-3998

Environmental Products (Indoor and Outdoor) and Services

PUR Portable Purifier (for water):

> Real Goods
> 555 Leslie Street
> Ukiah, CA 95482
> (800) 347-0070

Water quality testing/federal government's
Environmental Protection Agency:

> EPA Drinking Water Hotline: (800) 462-4791

Spot Check, pesticide test kit for food, water, lawn, garden:

> Environmental Health & Safety Products
> 3500 West 75th St., #304
> Prairie Village, KS 66208
> (800) 779-3477

Radon Testing: (800) SOS-RADON

Nontoxic gardening:

> Gardeners Supply
> 128 Intervale Rd.
> Burlington, VT 05401
> (802) 863-1700

Organic gardening:

> Johnny's Selected Seeds
> 299 Foss Hill Rd.
> Albion, ME 04910
> (207) 437-9294

Shepherd's Garden Seeds
30 Irene St.
Torrington, CT 06790
(203) 482-3638

Environmental Organizations

Clean Water Action: (202) 457-1286

National Coalition Against Misuse of Pesticides (MCAMP): (202) 543-5450

Earthwatch
680 Mt. Auburn St.
Box 403 N
Watertown, MA 02272
(800) 776-0188

Nontoxic Hair and Beauty Salons

Daryl Christopher Salon & Day Spa
37 Newberry St.
Boston, MA 02116
(617) 424-0250; call for names and locations of similar salons in your area

Herbal and Botanical Products, Organic Foods, Nutritional Supplements

Organic Planet (organic Chinese herbs)
430 West 24th St., #1-D
New York, NY 10011
(800) 627-3631; Call or write for mail order

Organic Coffee:

The Organic Coffee Co.: (800) 758-5282
Equal Exchange: (617) 344-7227
Cafe Altura: (805) 933-3027

Garlic Hotline
New York Hospital/Cornell Medical Center
(800) 330-5922; Monday–Friday, 9:00 A.M.–5:00 P.M.
Eastern time, for questions about the medicinal use of
garlic; will send free brochure

Sells nationwide guide to organic produce:

Community Alliance with Family Farmers (CAFF):
(916) 756-8518

Mountain Rose Herbs: (800) 879-3337

Herb & Spice: (800) 786-1388

Japanese and Chinese herbs, botanicals, marine botanicals,
essential oils, and supplies:

Frontier Direct
Box 127
Norway, IA 52318
(800) 726-5404

Japanese, macrobiotic and other organic foods, herbs,
botanicals, ingredients, and supplies:

Gold Mine Natural Food Company
1947 30th St.
San Diego, CA 92102
(800) 475-2000

Herb Products Company
11012 Magnolia Blvd.
North Hollywood, CA 81601

Mountain Ark Trading Company
120 South East Ave.
Fayetteville, AR 72701
(800) 643-8909

Sage Mountain Herbal Center
Box 420
East Barre, VT 05649
(802) 479-9825; call or write for information

Holistic Health Centers

The following have integrated mainstream and alternative medicine in a health center or hospital setting and can also refer you to a center in your area.

American Holistic Centers
990 West Fullerton Ave., #300
Chicago, IL 60614
(312) 296-6700; three centers in Chicago area

Arizona Center for Health & Medicine
5055 North 32 St., #200
Phoenix, AZ 85018
(602) 954-7400

Chopra Center for Well-Being
7590 Fay Avenue, #403
La Jolla, CA 92037
(619) 551-7788

Mind/Body Institute of Harvard Medical School
New England Deaconess Hospital
Hope Avenue
Waltham, MA 02254
(617) 647-6000

Spence Center for Women's Health
Charles Square
5 Bennett Street
Cambridge, MA 02138
(617) 661-3300

Women to Women
One Pleasant Street
Yarmouth, ME 04096
(207) 846-6163

Hormone Products

The following pharmaceutical companies make plant-derived natural estrogen, which can be prescribed by your physician and purchased at pharmacies:

COMPANY	PRODUCT NAME	SOURCE
Bristol Myers	Estrace	yam and soybeans
CIBA	Estraderm	sweet potatoes
Solovay	Estratab	soybeans
SmithKlineBeecham	Menest	Mexican yams and barbasco
Upjohn	Ogen	various vegetable sources

Plant-derived, natural estrogen and progesterone prescription drugs can be ordered by your physician from:

Women's International Pharmacy: (800) 279-5708

Medical and Healing Organizations

The following organizations can provide lists of member physicians
and practitioners in your area, as well as other information:

Academy for Guided Imagery
  Box 2070
  Mill Valley, CA 94942
  (415) 389-9324

American Academy of Medical Acupuncture
  5820 Wilshire Blvd., #500
  Los Angeles, CA 90036
  (213) 937-5514

American Academy of Osteopathy
  3500 De Pauw Blvd., #1080
  Indianapolis, IN 46268
  (317) 879-1881

American Aromatherapy Association
  Box 1222
  Fair Oaks, CA 95628

American Association of Acupuncture & Oriental Medicine
  433 Front St.
  Catasauqua, PA 18032
  (610) 266-1433

American Association of Naturopathic Physicians
  2366 Eastlake Ave., East
  Suite 322
  Seattle, WA 98102
  (206) 328-8510

American Foundation of Traditional Chinese Medicine
505 Beach St.
San Francisco, CA 94133
(415) 776-0502

American Herbalists Guild
Box 1683
Soquel, CA 95073
(408) 464-2441

American Holistic Medical Association
4101 Lake Boone Trail, #201
Raleigh, NC 27607
(919) 787-5146

American Massage Therapy Association
820 Davies St., #100
Evanston, IL 60201
(847) 864-0123

Associated Bodywork & Massage Professionals
28677 Buffalo Park Rd.
Evergreen, CO 80439
(800) 458-2267

Association of Natural Medicine Pharmacists
(707) 887-1351; provides pharmacists with up-to-date
scientific information on natural medicines

Feldenkreis Guild of North America
Box 489
Albany, OR 97231
(800) 775-2118

International Healing Tao Centers
   Box 1194
   Huntington, NY 11743
   (516) 367-2701

National Center for Homeopathy
   801 N. Fairfax St., #306
   Alexandria, VA 22134
   (703) 548-7790

Rolf Institute
   205 Canyon Blvd.
   Boulder, CO 80306
   (303) 449-5903

The Seymour System
   1865 79th Street Causeway, Suite 14-N
   North Bay Village, FL 33141
   (305) 623-6360

Selected Bibliography and Suggested Reading

To keep your eyes from glazing over as you read a long list of books and publications, I've organized this portion of Resources into topic categories. Some topics overlap, of course. For instance, all of the books in the Ayurvedic Medicine, Women's, Men's, and Travel categories are just as natural and body-mind-spirit-oriented as those in the larger Natural Medicine and Treatments for Body, Mind, and Spirit category. And we are reminded, even in this guide to resources, that *everything* is interconnected.

Ayurvedic Medicine

Chopra, Deepak, M.D. *Perfect Health*. New York: Harmony Books, 1991.

Chopra, Deepak, M.D. *Quantum Healing*. New York: Bantam Books, 1990.

Lonsdorf, Nancy, M.D.; Butler, Veronica, M.D.; and Brown, Melanie, Ph.D. *A Woman's Best Medicine: Health, Happiness and Long Life Through Ayur-Veda*. New York: Jeremy P. Tarcher/Putnam, 1993.

Sachs, Melanie. *Ayurvedic Beauty Care*. Silver Lake, WI: Lotus Press, 1994.

Tiwari, Maya. *Ayurveda: A Life of Balance*. Rochester, VT: Healing Arts Press, 1993.

Environment

Berthold-Bond, Annie. *Annie Berthold-Bond's Clean and Green.* Woodstock, NY: Ceres Press, 1990.

Dadd, Debra Lynn. *The Non-Toxic Home and Office.* New York: Jeremy P. Tarcher/Putnam, 1992.

Organic Gardening, monthly magazine, published by Rodale Press, Emmaus, PA.

Men

Kimbrell, Andrew. *The Masculine Mystique.* New York: Ballantine, 1995.

Travel

Fairchild, Diana. *Jet Smart.* Berkeley, CA: Celestial Arts, 1992.

Women

Blum, Jeanne Elizabeth. *Woman Heal Thyself.* Boston: Charles E. Tuttle, 1995. (Chinese Medicine)

Carlson, Karn J., M.D.; Eisenstat, Stephanie A., M.D.; and Ziporyn, Terra, Ph.D. *The Harvard Guide to Women's Health.* Cambridge: Harvard University Press, 1995.

Elias, Jason, and Ketcham, Katherine. *In the House of the Moon.* New York: Warner Books, 1995. (Chinese Medicine)

Gladstar, Rosemary. *Herbal Healing for Women.* New York: Simon & Schuster, 1993.

Hanley, Jesse Lynn, M.D. *Menopause: Dispelling the Myths, Telling the Truth, Exploring the Possibilities.* VHS Video. Moondance Productions, 4403 Mattos Drive, Fremont, CA 94534. (800) 760-7775. 1994.

Lark, Susan M., M.D. *PMS Self-Help Book.* Berkeley, CA: Celestial Arts, 1984.

Northrup, Christiane, M.D. *Women's Bodies, Women's Wisdom.* New York: Bantam Books, 1994.

Ojeda, Linda, Ph.D. *Menopause Without Medicine* (3d ed.). Alameda, CA: Hunter House, 1995.

Singer, Sydney Ross, and Gismaijer, Soma. *Dressed to Kill: The Link Between Breast Cancer and Bras.* Garden City Park, NY: Avery, 1993.

Wolfe, Honora Lee. *Menopause, A Second Spring: Making a Smooth Transition with Chinese Medicine.* Boulder, CO: Blue Poppy Press, 1995.

Journeys of Body, Mind, and Spirit

Ascher, Barbara. *Landscape Without Gravity: A Memoir of Grief.* Harrison, NY: Delphinium, 1992.

Chiles, Pila. *The Secrets and Mysteries of Hawaii.* Deerfield Beach, FL: Health Communications, 1995.

Medicine Eagle, Brooke. *Buffalo Woman Comes Singing.* New York: Ballantine, 1991.

Millman, Dan. *Way of the Peaceful Warrior.* Tiburon, CA: H. J. Kramer, 1984.

Redfield, James. *The Celestine Prophecy.* New York: Warner Books, 1994.

Redfield, James. *The Tenth Insight.* New York: Warner Books, 1996.

Rossbach, Sarah. *Feng Shui: The Chinese Art of Placement.* New York: Arkana/Penguin, 1991.

Sanchez, Victor. *The Teachings of Don Carlos.* Santa Fe: Bear & Co., 1995.

Talbot, Michael. *The Holographic Universe.* New York: Harper-Collins, 1991.

Weiss, Brian L., M.D. *Many Lives, Many Masters.* New York: Simon & Schuster, 1988.

Weiss, Brian L., M.D. *Through Time into Healing.* New York: Simon & Schuster. 1992.

Wolf, Fred Alan. *The Eagle's Quest.* New York: Summit Books, 1991.

Zukav, Gary. *The Seat of the Soul.* Simon & Schuster, 1990.

Natural Medicine and Treatments for Body, Mind, and Spirit

Antol, Marie Nadine. *Healing Teas: A Practical Guide to the Medicinal Teas of the World.* Garden City Park, NY: Avery, 1996.

Borysenko, Joan, M.D. *The Power of the Mind to Heal.* Carson, CA: Hay House, 1994.

Braly, James, M.D. *Dr. Braly's Food Allergy and Nutrition Revolution.* New Canaan, CT: Keats Publishing, 1992.

Brennan, Barbara. *Hands of Light: A Guide to Healing Through the Human Energy Field.* New York: Bantam Books, 1988.

Brennan, Barbara. *Light Emerging: A Journey of Personal Healing.* New York: Bantam Books, 1993.

Chia, Mantak. *Awaken Healing Energy Through the Tao.* Santa Fe: Aurora Press, 1983.

Chopra, Deepak, M.D. *Unconditional Life,* New York: Bantam Books, 1992.

Chopra, Deepak, M.D. *Ageless Body, Timeless Mind.* New York: Harmony Books, 1993.

Conway, Amy. *Nature's Beauty Box.* Boston: Charles E. Tuttle, 1995.

Douillard, John. *Body, Mind & Sport.* New York: Harmony Books, 1994.

Fertman, John. *Hands-On Healing: Massage Remedies for Hundreds of Health Problems.* Emmaus, PA: Rodale Press, 1989.

Foster, Steven. *Echinacea.* Rochester, VT: Healing Arts Press, 1991.

Gerber, Richard, M.D. *Vibrational Medicine* (rev. ed.), Santa Fe: Bear & Co., 1988.

Howard, Judy. *The Bach Flower Remedies: Step by Step.* Essex, England: C. W. Daniel, 1991.

Keville, Kathi. *Aromatherapy: A Complete Guide to the Healing Art.* Freedom, CA: Crossing Press, 1995.

Kloss, Jethro. *Back to Eden: The Classic Guide to Herbal Medicine, Natural Foods and Home Remedies.* Loma Linda, CA: Back to Eden Books, 1992.

Leigh, Michelle Dominique. *Inner Peace, Outer Beauty: Natural Japanese Health and Beauty Secrets Revealed.* New York: Citadel Press, 1995.

Lieberman, Jacob, O.D., Ph.D. *Light: Medicine of the Future.* Santa Fe: Bear & Co., 1991.

Moyers, Bill. *Healing and the Mind.* New York: Doubleday, 1993.

Pizzorno, Joe, N.D., and Murray, Michael, N.D. *Encyclopedia of Natural Medicine.* Rocklin, CA: Prima Publishing, 1991.

Somer, Elizabeth. *The Essential Guide to Vitamins and Minerals.* New York: HarperCollins, 1995.

Sonberg, Lynn. *The Health Nutrient Bible.* New York: Fireside/Simon & Schuster, 1995.

Tierra, Michael. *The Way of Herbs.* New York: Pocket Books, 1990.

Ullman, Dana, M.P.H. *The Consumers Guide to Homeopathy.* New York: Jeremy P. Tarcher/Putnam, 1991.

Weil, Andrew, M.D. *Spontaneous Healing.* New York: Knopf, 1995.

Weil, Andrew, M.D. *Natural Health, Natural Medicine* (rev. ed.). New York: Houghton Mifflin, 1995.

Weil, Andrew, M.D. *Health and Healing* (rev. ed.). New York: Houghton Mifflin, 1995.

Worwood, Valerie Ann. *The Complete Book of Essential Oils & Aromatherapy.* San Rafael, CA: New World Library, 1991.

Publications and Periodicals

Natural Health, bimonthly magazine. Subscriptions: P.O. Box 7440, Red Oak, IA 51591. (800) 526-8440. Editorial office: 17 Station Street, Box 1200, Brookline Village, MA 02147.

Alternative Therapies in Health and Medicine, A Peer-Reviewed Journal. Bimonthly. Subscriptions: (800) 345-8112. Editorial office: 101 Columbia, Aliso Viejo, CA 92656. (800) 899-1712.

HerbalGram, Journal of the American Botanical Council and the Herbal Research Foundation. For information: Box 201660, Austin, TX. (512) 331-8868. Also, the Botanical Council has a bookstore in Austin. For information and orders: (800) 373-7105.

Index

About the Author

Nina L. Diamond is a journalist and essayist whose work has appeared in *Omni, The Miami Herald*'s *Health Beat, The Chicago Tribune,* and more than fifty other magazines and newspapers. She has extensively covered science, medicine, natural health, metaphysics, the arts, current affairs, and books, and has published social satire, humor, and essays.

She is the editor of *Deepak Chopra's Infinite Well-Being for Body, Mind & Soul,* a writer and performer on National Public Radio's *Pandemonium,* and a contemporary composer and pianist whose debut album of piano solos, *New Places,* will be released in 1997 by Serenada Records. She lives in South Florida.